REMARKABLE

A 40-DAY JOURNEY THROUGH
THE BOOK OF MARK

MARGARET FEINBERG

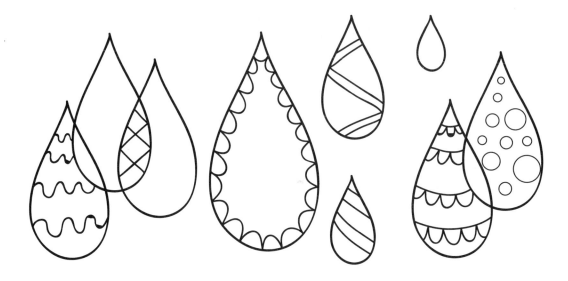

REMARKABLE

A 40-DAY JOURNEY THROUGH
THE BOOK OF MARK

A LETTER FROM MARGARET

Sometimes we can lose sight of the remarkable nature of Jesus Christ. The teachings. The miracles. The presence. The writer of the Gospel of Mark reminds us of the beauty of Christ in a concise, thoughtful book. The smallest of the four Gospels, Mark doesn't waste time or words as he jettisons readers through the life, death, and resurrection of Jesus. More than anything, Mark wants the life of Christ to become our life.

Remarkable provides a 40-day journey into the Gospel of Mark. Each day is coupled with a devotional entry and reflection questions. Through the upcoming pages, you'll discover a better way to live through Jesus Christ.

Grab a handful of colored pencils, markers, or crayons to slow down as you read Scripture. Take time to circle the verbs, underline the names, and consider the details of the text as you doodle and reflect. Gather around the table. Invite a friend, your kids, or your grandkids to join.

My prayer is that during this time you'll awaken to Jesus and the wonder of Scripture, and you'll live out your faith in a more radiant and remarkable way.

Together, let's learn to know the Remarkable One.

Blessings,
Margaret

THE COLOR METHOD

Creativity splashes in my readings of Scripture. I'm learning to let my inner doodler dance and play. I scribble like a 4-year-old, but the swirls and colors provide time for the words and the phrases to sink deeper into my soul.

Coloring slows our pace.
Coloring highlights the patterns, repeated words, and holy emphasis.
Coloring invites us beyond reading the Scripture and invites the Scripture to read us.

Most days' readings in *Remarkable* take a handful of minutes. Adding the Color Method will double or triple your study time as you read through each portion of Scripture several times. The depth, the richness, the discoveries make this extra effort worth every moment.

Here is what I do with the different colors:

Circle verbs in **red** to highlight the activity of God and people.
Circle places in **brown** to note location.
Circle names in **purple** to identify people.
Mark numbers in **orange** to identify numerals and quantities.
Mark the Holy Spirit, angels, and the prophetic in **blue** to identify God's presence and handiwork.
Scribble observations in your **favorite colors** to record insights.

Bonus Challenge: The Gospel of Mark uses the word "euthus" over 40 times. "Euthus" translates as immediately, directly, straightway, at once, shortly, or forthwith. Star each occurance of one of these translations in **yellow**. Why do you think Mark uses this word so often?

Following the Scripture reading, you'll find a devotion that zeroes in on one concept from the passage. I wrote these to spur your thoughts and hearts Christward. Each day's reading closes with reflection questions designed for personal or small group use.

As you finish studying each day, consider how you can respond in an active way. You may be nudged to prayer, repentance, a generous act, or a kind word. Ask God how you can be both a hearer and a doer of the day's reading.

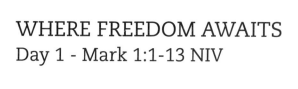

WHERE FREEDOM AWAITS
Day 1 - Mark 1:1-13 NIV

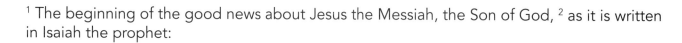

¹ The beginning of the good news about Jesus the Messiah, the Son of God, ² as it is written in Isaiah the prophet:

"I will send my messenger ahead of you, who will prepare your way"—³ "a voice of one calling in the wilderness, 'Prepare the way for the Lord, make straight paths for him.'"

⁴ And so John the Baptist appeared in the wilderness, preaching a baptism of repentance for the forgiveness of sins. ⁵ The whole Judean countryside and all the people of Jerusalem went out to him. Confessing their sins, they were baptized by him in the Jordan River.

⁶ John wore clothing made of camel's hair, with a leather belt around his waist, and he ate locusts and wild honey. ⁷ And this was his message: "After me comes the one more powerful than I, the straps of whose sandals I am not worthy to stoop down and untie. ⁸ I baptize you with water, but he will baptize you with the Holy Spirit."

⁹ At that time Jesus came from Nazareth in Galilee and was baptized by John in the Jordan. ¹⁰ Just as Jesus was coming up out of the water, he saw heaven being torn open and the Spirit descending on him like a dove. ¹¹ And a voice came from heaven: "You are my Son, whom I love; with you I am well pleased."

¹² At once the Spirit sent him out into the wilderness, ¹³ and he was in the wilderness forty days, being tempted by Satan. He was with the wild animals, and angels attended him.

John the Immerser appears weathered. Sunburned crow's feet march around his eyes double time. Despite the ache in his back and pangs in his stomach, neither his voice nor his message waivers: Repent.

Wealthy men don wool and ornate belts. John's dress includes scratchy camel hair and a leather belt. He's enrobed in the clothes of the poor. John awaits to immerse any man, woman, or child willing to confess their failings to follow the law—the Torah—and live upright before God.

For John, only the Remarkable One is above reproach and has no reason for baptism. But Jesus insists, and all heaven tosses a party that day.

The Spirit nudges Jesus into the wilderness to face great temptation. That's a fast change from heaven to hell. Cool waters and descending doves are replaced with heat and hunger.

#RemarkableStudy

This grueling triathlon of temptation becomes the launching pad for Jesus' ministry. He did what we could not. And do you know the first message Jesus preached? Repent.

Jesus triumphs over temptation so we can too.

John set Jesus up well. And Jesus set us up well by teaching us that there's no temptation we will face that Christ has not overcome. That's really good news.

1. Where are you being tempted most in your life?
2. How has God provided you a way of escape?
3. What steps do you need to take to rise above this temptation?
4. Using the Color Method, what stood out to you most from today's Scripture?

WHEN GOD INTERRUPTS YOUR DAY
Day 2 - Mark 1:14-28 NKJV

[14] Now after John was put in prison, Jesus came to Galilee, preaching the gospel of the kingdom of God, [15] and saying, "The time is fulfilled, and the kingdom of God is at hand. Repent, and believe in the gospel."

[16] And as He walked by the Sea of Galilee, He saw Simon and Andrew his brother casting a net into the sea; for they were fishermen. [17] Then Jesus said to them, "Follow Me, and I will make you become fishers of men."

[18] They immediately left their nets and followed Him. [19] When He had gone a little farther from there, He saw James the son of Zebedee, and John his brother, who also were in the boat mending their nets. [20] And immediately He called them, and they left their father Zebedee in the boat with the hired servants, and went after Him.

[21] Then they went into Capernaum, and immediately on the Sabbath He entered the synagogue and taught. [22] And they were astonished at His teaching, for He taught them as one having authority, and not as the scribes.

[23] Now there was a man in their synagogue with an unclean spirit. And he cried out, [24] saying, "Let us alone! What have we to do with You, Jesus of Nazareth? Did You come to destroy us? I know who You are—the Holy One of God!"

[25] But Jesus rebuked him, saying, "Be quiet, and come out of him!" [26] And when the unclean spirit had convulsed him and cried out with a loud voice, he came out of him. [27] Then they were all amazed, so that they questioned among themselves, saying, "What is this? What new doctrine is this? For with authority He commands even the unclean spirits, and they obey Him." [28] And immediately His fame spread throughout all the region around Galilee.

Simon and Andrew focus on casting their nets when Jesus interrupts, "Follow Me, and I will become fishers of men." In essence, Jesus says, "What you're doing is good, but I've got something remarkably better." With those words, *BAM*, two disciples begin following Jesus.

James and John focus on mending their nets when Jesus interrupts. Jesus calls them and, *BAM*, they follow Jesus, too.

Then, a tormented man appears in the synagogue. Jesus interrupts again by banishing the unclean spirit. Though these men are focused in different directions—casting, mending, being tormented— Jesus meets each one, interrupts their lives, and ushers them into greater purpose and freedom.

Unexpected interruptions are God's remarkable invitations.

No matter your focus of the day—in work or life—look for Jesus' interruption. They represent opportunities for God to display remarkable love and power in your life.

#RemarkableStudy

1. Do you view interruptions as obstacles or opportunities? Explain.

2. Describe when you have been interrupted by God most recently.

3. How do divine interruptions heighten your awareness of God's presence?

4. Using the Color Method, what stood out to you most from today's Scripture?

LET THIS MOVE YOU
Day 3 - Mark 1:29-45 HCSB

29 As soon as they left the synagogue, they went into Simon and Andrew's house with James and John. 30 Simon's mother-in-law was lying in bed with a fever, and they told Him about her at once. 31 So He went to her, took her by the hand, and raised her up. The fever left her, and she began to serve them.

32 When evening came, after the sun had set, they began bringing to Him all those who were sick and those who were demon-possessed. 33 The whole town was assembled at the door, 34 and He healed many who were sick with various diseases and drove out many demons. But He would not permit the demons to speak, because they knew Him.

35 Very early in the morning, while it was still dark, He got up, went out, and made His way to a deserted place. And He was praying there. 36 Simon and his companions went searching for Him. 37 They found Him and said, "Everyone's looking for You!"

38 And He said to them, "Let's go on to the neighboring villages so that I may preach there too. This is why I have come." 39 So He went into all of Galilee, preaching in their synagogues and driving out demons.

40 Then a man with a serious skin disease came to Him and, on his knees, begged Him: "If You are willing, You can make me clean."

41 Moved with compassion, Jesus reached out His hand and touched him. "I am willing," He told him. "Be made clean." 42 Immediately the disease left him, and he was healed. 43 Then He sternly warned him and sent him away at once, 44 telling him, "See that you say nothing to anyone; but go and show yourself to the priest, and offer what Moses prescribed for your cleansing, as a testimony to them."45 Yet he went out and began to proclaim it widely and to spread the news, with the result that Jesus could no longer enter a town openly. But He was out in deserted places, and they would come to Him from everywhere.

The Anointed One drips with healing and splashes the cool waters of the kingdom of God in all directions. To those who will receive. To those who are willing. To those who are hungry and thirsty.

Jesus returns from a deserted place only to have a man with leprosy kneel before Him and request the impossible. Make him whole. Make him clean. Make him new again. Jesus reaches, touches, speaks, and the disease disappears forever.

Three remarkable words nestle before Jesus' powerful response:

Moved. With. Compassion.

Jesus doesn't heal for the accolades, the attention, or the sense of accomplishment. Jesus doesn't heal to prove or placate or people-please. From Christ's words and deeds, we learn:

Divine healing always commences with compassion.

In every situation in which you find yourself today, in every encounter, may you be moved with the compassion of Christ.

1. Where do you ache to experience healing most?
2. Describe a time when you experienced healing from God.
3. How do aches, pains, and discomfort help you recognize your need for God?
4. Using the Color Method, what stood out to you most from today's Scripture?

HOW TO BE A REMARKABLE FRIEND
Day 4 - Mark 2:1-13 MSG

1-5 After a few days, Jesus returned to Capernaum, and word got around that he was back home. A crowd gathered, jamming the entrance so no one could get in or out. He was teaching the Word. They brought a paraplegic to him, carried by four men. When they weren't able to get in because of the crowd, they removed part of the roof and lowered the paraplegic on his stretcher. Impressed by their bold belief, Jesus said to the paraplegic, "Son, I forgive your sins."

6-7 Some religion scholars sitting there started whispering among themselves, "He can't talk that way! That's blasphemy! God and only God can forgive sins."

8-12 Jesus knew right away what they were thinking, and said, "Why are you so skeptical? Which is simpler: to say to the paraplegic, 'I forgive your sins,' or say, 'Get up, take your stretcher, and start walking'? Well, just so it's clear that I'm the Son of Man and authorized to do either, or both…" (he looked now at the paraplegic), "Get up. Pick up your stretcher and go home." And the man did it—got up, grabbed his stretcher, and walked out, with everyone there watching him. They rubbed their eyes, incredulous—and then praised God, saying, "We've never seen anything like this!"

13 Then Jesus went again to walk alongside the lake. Again a crowd came to him, and he taught them.

Jesus performs a profound miracle when a paraplegic grabs his stretcher and takes his first steps. But have you stopped to consider…

The remarkable role of the man's friends?

Or rather…

The remarkable role you can play in the lives of your friends?

You can play a remarkable role in the healing of your friends. Sometimes you have to cut holes in impossible situations, break through the it-can't-be-done, and believe for others when they're ready to give up.

Sometimes you're the one God uses to carry a person over the finish line, walk the person down the aisle, spur the friend to take that bucket list adventure. You're the one who reaches down, scoops up, and refuses to let go. You're the one who declares through your words and deeds, "You don't get to quit." You're the one who, despite all odds, keeps bringing the person to Jesus.

Remarkable friends trust in a remarkable God.

The remarkable friends of the paralytic remind us that when we carry our friends and their burdens, we play a crucial role in their healing.

1. Who is someone God is nudging you to help carry now?
2. Have you ever carried someone and seen a miracle as a result? Explain.
3. List three ways you can give the gift of your presence to someone in need today.
4. Using the Color Method, what stood out to you most from today's Scripture?

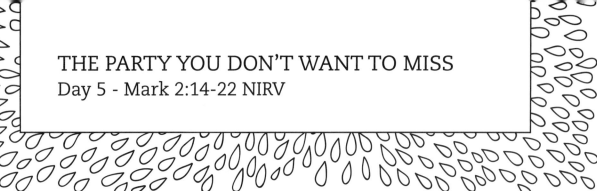

14 As he walked along he saw Levi, the son of Alphaeus.

Levi was sitting at the tax collector's booth. "Follow me," Jesus told him. Levi got up and followed him.

15 Later Jesus was having dinner at Levi's house. Many tax collectors and sinners were eating with him and his disciples. They were part of the large crowd following Jesus.

16 Some teachers of the law who were Pharisees were there.

They saw Jesus eating with sinners and tax collectors.

So they asked his disciples, "Why does he eat with tax collectors and sinners?"

17 Jesus heard that. So he said to them, "Those who are healthy don't need a doctor. Sick people do. I have not come to get those who think they are right with God to follow me. I have come to get sinners to follow me."

18 John's disciples and the Pharisees were going without eating. Some people came to Jesus.

They said to him, "John's disciples are fasting. The disciples of the Pharisees are also fasting. But your disciples are not. Why aren't they?"

19 Jesus answered, "How can the guests of the groom go without eating while he is with them? They will not fast as long as he is with them.

20 But the time will come when the groom will be taken away from them. On that day they will go without eating.

21 "No one sews a patch of new cloth on old clothes. Otherwise, the new piece will pull away from the old. That will make the tear worse.

22 No one pours new wine into old wineskins. Otherwise, the wine will burst the skins.

Then the wine and the wineskins will both be destroyed. No, people pour new wine into new wineskins."

Elite. Rich. Middle-class. Poor. Elderly. Young and naïve. Baby boomer. Millennial. Felon. Sex addict. Surgically enhanced. Botoxed and Juvadermed. Refugee. Foreigner. Widow. Orphan. User. Gambler. Short. Tall. Obese. Skeleton-thin. Scantily clad. Homeschooler. Ivy Leaguer.

Our biases betray us. We aren't the only ones.

Levi throws a shindig, and his house soon fills wall-to-wall with Jesus followers. The guest list raises suspicion and spurs whispers among the religious leaders. Sinners and tax collectors. Why would anyone of top repute break bread with the bottom feeders?

Those are the exact people Jesus has come to rescue. Those the religious leaders mark as left-behind losers, Christ marks as remarkably redeemed.

When it comes to liars and smugglers and murderers, Jesus shouts, "Everyone's welcome at redemption's table."

That's good news for you and me because there's plenty of room for us. But that also means we must make plenty of room for them. "Them" who look different, "them" who talk different, "them" who walk different, "them" who smell different, "them" who live different.

Our biases always betray, but when we lock eyes with Jesus, they melt away.

1. What biases and prejudices do you struggle with most?
2. Who are you tempted to write off, dismiss, exclude from the Jesus invite list?
3. What steps can you take to see others as Jesus sees them?
4. Using the Color Method, what stood out to you most from today's Scripture?

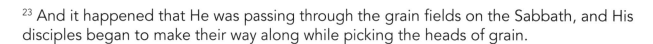
23 And it happened that He was passing through the grain fields on the Sabbath, and His disciples began to make their way along while picking the heads of grain.

24 The Pharisees were saying to Him, "Look, why are they doing what is not lawful on the Sabbath?"

25 And He said to them, "Have you never read what David did when he was in need and he and his companions became hungry; 26 how he entered the house of God in the time of Abiathar the high priest, and ate the consecrated bread, which is not lawful for anyone to eat except the priests, and he also gave it to those who were with him?"

27 Jesus said to them, "The Sabbath was made for man, and not man for the Sabbath. 28 So the Son of Man is Lord even of the Sabbath."

3 ¹He entered again into a synagogue; and a man was there whose hand was withered. 2 They were watching Him to see if He would heal him on the Sabbath, so that they might accuse Him.

3 He said to the man with the withered hand, "Get up and come forward!" 4 And He said to them, "Is it lawful to do good or to do harm on the Sabbath, to save a life or to kill?" But they kept silent.

5 After looking around at them with anger, grieved at their hardness of heart, He said to the man, "Stretch out your hand." And he stretched it out, and his hand was restored. 6 The Pharisees went out and immediately began conspiring with the Herodians against Him, as to how they might destroy Him.

7 Jesus withdrew to the sea with His disciples; and a great multitude from Galilee followed; and also from Judea, 8 and from Jerusalem, and from Idumea, and beyond the Jordan, and the vicinity of Tyre and Sidon, a great number of people heard of all that He was doing and came to Him.

9 And He told His disciples that a boat should stand ready for Him because of the crowd, so that they would not crowd Him; 10 for He had healed many, with the result that all those who had afflictions pressed around Him in order to touch Him.

11 Whenever the unclean spirits saw Him, they would fall down before Him and shout, "You are the Son of God!" 12 And He earnestly warned them not to tell who He was.

Jesus conflicts with the religious establishment over the Sabbath. Why is this such a major sticking point? Because the religious leaders think Jesus questions the authority of the Torah. The irony: Jesus *is* the authority of the Torah.

In back-to-back stories, Jesus answers questions regarding the Sabbath. In the process, He teaches the religious leaders and us:

There's never a bad day to do something really good.

In the process, Jesus shows us the Sabbath is a remarkable day. The purpose of the Sabbath isn't what's done or left undone as much as breathing and exhaling the goodness of God. The more you breathe in, the more you'll long for another breath. The Sabbath invites us to live wide-eyed for God to work something remarkable in us and through us.

If we allow, the Sabbath is a gift through which we slow down so we once again become wonderstruck by the goodness of God in our lives, relationships, and world. The Sabbath provides the opportunity to nurture our appreciation for the beauty of creation, the deliciousness of provision, the joy of celebration. And all that goodness is meant to be shared with others.

1. When during the week do you inhale and exhale the goodness of God?
2. What does Sabbath look like for you?
3. In what area do you need to practice grace instead of judgment?
4. Using the Color Method, what stood out to you most from today's Scripture?

HOW TO JOIN THE GREATEST FAMILY
Day 7 - Mark 3:13-35 PHILLIPS

13-19 Later he went up on to the hill-side and summoned the men whom he wanted, and they went up to him. He appointed a band of twelve to be his companions, whom he could send out to preach, with power to drive out evil spirits.

These were the twelve he appointed: Peter (which was the new name he gave Simon), James the son of Zebedee, and John his brother (He gave them the name of Boanerges, which means the "Thunderers".) Andrew, Philip, Bartholomew, Matthew, Thomas, James the son of Alphaeus, Thaddaeus, Simon the Patriot, and Judas Iscariot, who betrayed him.

20-21 Then he went indoors, but again such a crowd collected that it was impossible for them even to eat a meal. When his relatives heard of this, they set out to take charge of him, for people were saying, "He must be mad!"

22-27 The scribes who had come down from Jerusalem were saying that he was possessed by Beelzebub, and that he drove out devils because he was in league with the prince of devils.

So Jesus called them to him and spoke to them in a parable—"How can Satan be the one who drives out Satan? If a kingdom is divided against itself, it cannot last either. And if Satan leads a rebellion against Satan—his days are certainly numbered. No one can break into a strong man's house and steal his property, without first tying up the strong man hand and foot. But if he did that, he could ransack the whole house.

28-29 "Believe me, all men's sins can be forgiven and their blasphemies. But there can never be any forgiveness for blasphemy against the Holy Spirit. That is an eternal sin."

30 He said this because they were saying, "He is in the power of an evil spirit."

31-32 Then his mother and his brothers arrived. They stood outside the house and sent a message asking him to come out to them.

There was a crowd sitting round him when the message was brought telling him, "Your mother and your brothers are outside looking for you."

33 Jesus replied, "And who are really my mother and my brothers?"

34 And he looked round at the faces of those sitting in a circle about him. 35 "Look!" he said, "my mother and my brothers are here. Anyone who does the will of God is brother and sister and mother to me."

In Mark's account, when Jesus designates the dirty dozen known as the disciples, He climbs a mountain and invites the followers to climb, too.

The Ultimate Ascent invites His followers to ascend. To rise above. To push through. After all, the climb won't always be easy. Muscles fatigue. Lungs strain. Hands scramble to grip.

Jesus' invitation to climb foreshadows His followers' upcoming spiritual journey.

The disciples will soon find themselves trekking to hard and difficult places. Crowded homes with no time to eat. Interactions where leaders spread rumors and scholars slather slander.

When Jesus' mother and brothers arrive, one might suspect them to enjoy a hearty greeting. Receive priority. Top billing. Preferential treatment.

Yet Jesus says obedience runs thicker than blood. When you follow Jesus wherever He leads:

You're more than a follower, you're family.

Those who answer the call to climb with Christ and walk in obedience are God's family. How do you make this trek with the Remarkable One? One obedient step at a time.

1. Draw a picture of the geographical terrain that describes your faith journey.
2. How would you describe the spiritual steepness of your life right now?
3. In what area of your life is it hardest to walk in obedience?
4. Using the Color Method, what stood out to you most from today's Scripture?

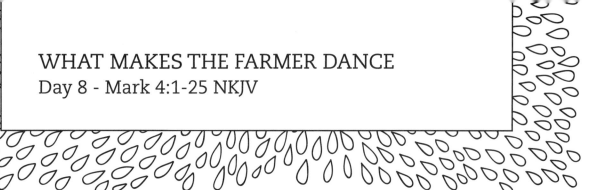
[1] And again He began to teach by the sea. And a great multitude was gathered to Him, so that He got into a boat and sat in it on the sea; and the whole multitude was on the land facing the sea. [2] Then He taught them many things by parables, and said to them in His teaching:

[3] "Listen! Behold, a sower went out to sow. [4] And it happened, as he sowed, that some seed fell by the wayside; and the birds of the air came and devoured it. [5] Some fell on stony ground, where it did not have much earth; and immediately it sprang up because it had no depth of earth. [6] But when the sun was up it was scorched, and because it had no root it withered away. [7] And some seed fell among thorns; and the thorns grew up and choked it, and it yielded no crop. [8] But other seed fell on good ground and yielded a crop that sprang up, increased and produced: some thirtyfold, some sixty, and some a hundred."

[9] And He said to them, "He who has ears to hear, let him hear!"

[10] But when He was alone, those around Him with the twelve asked Him about the parable. [11] And He said to them, "To you it has been given to know the mystery of the kingdom of God; but to those who are outside, all things come in parables,[12] so that 'Seeing they may see and not perceive, And hearing they may hear and not understand; Lest they should turn, And their sins be forgiven them.'"

[13] And He said to them, "Do you not understand this parable? How then will you understand all the parables? [14] The sower sows the word. [15] And these are the ones by the wayside where the word is sown. When they hear, Satan comes immediately and takes away the word that was sown in their hearts. [16] These likewise are the ones sown on stony ground who, when they hear the word, immediately receive it with gladness; [17] and they have no root in themselves, and so endure only for a time. Afterward, when tribulation or persecution arises for the word's sake, immediately they stumble.

[18] Now these are the ones sown among thorns; they are the ones who hear the word, [19] and the cares of this world, the deceitfulness of riches, and the desires for other things entering in choke the word, and it becomes unfruitful. [20] But these are the ones sown on good ground, those who hear the word, accept it, and bear fruit: some thirtyfold, some sixty, and some a hundred."

[21] Also He said to them, "Is a lamp brought to be put under a basket or under a bed? Is it not to be set on a lampstand? [22] For there is nothing hidden which will not be revealed, nor has anything been kept secret but that it should come to light. [23] If anyone has ears to hear, let him hear."

²⁴ Then He said to them, "Take heed what you hear. With the same measure you use, it will be measured to you; and to you who hear, more will be given. ²⁵ For whoever has, to him more will be given; but whoever does not have, even what he has will be taken away from him."

In Mark 4, Jesus stacks story on story and presses listeners to attentiveness: "Are you listening to this? Really listening?"

The stories are gifts, but they are also enigmas. The moment we think we understand, the Holy Spirit uncovers a different facet of meaning, a new way to encounter them, to encounter Him, and for them to encounter us. These are not stories of old, but fresh stories meant to awaken our hearts to God every day.

Jesus tells the story of a farmer who scatters seed. Of the precious grain, some falls. Some lands. Some casts. Then some birds consume. Gravel chokes. Weeds strangle.

No one understands. Jesus tugs His followers-turned-family into a huddle to unfold the treasures of the story. In the process, He reveals our cement hearts and shallow roots. He identifies what chokes the God-life from our bones. Then, He reveals where God takes pleasure.

The Farmer dances when He sees the work of the Remarkable One in you.

Unlike the seeds plucked away, the Farmer dances when He sees you and me, the people in whom the embryos of Christ are planted, flourish, multiply, and yield an abundant harvest.

1. What's circling in your life, plucking away your hope and trust?
2. What gravel chips are stunting your ability to grow deeper spiritually or relationally?
3. What thistles, if not removed, will soon take over your heart?
4. Using the Color Method, what stood out to you most from today's Scripture?

WHEN GOD SAYS "HUSH"
Day 9 - Mark 4:26-41 NASB

26 And He was saying, "The kingdom of God is like a man who casts seed upon the soil; 27 and he goes to bed at night and gets up by day, and the seed sprouts and grows—how, he himself does not know.

28 The soil produces crops by itself; first the blade, then the head, then the mature grain in the head. 29 But when the crop permits, he immediately puts in the sickle, because the harvest has come."

30 And He said, "How shall we picture the kingdom of God, or by what parable shall we present it?

31 It is like a mustard seed, which, when sown upon the soil, though it is smaller than all the seeds that are upon the soil, 32 yet when it is sown, it grows up and becomes larger than all the garden plants and forms large branches; so that the birds of the air can nest under its shade."

33 With many such parables He was speaking the word to them, so far as they were able to hear it; 34 and He did not speak to them without a parable; but He was explaining everything privately to His own disciples.

35 On that day, when evening came, He said to them, "Let us go over to the other side."

36 Leaving the crowd, they took Him along with them in the boat, just as He was; and other boats were with Him.

37 And there arose a fierce gale of wind, and the waves were breaking over the boat so much that the boat was already filling up.

38 Jesus Himself was in the stern, asleep on the cushion; and they woke Him and said to Him, "Teacher, do You not care that we are perishing?"

39 And He got up and rebuked the wind and said to the sea, "Hush, be still." And the wind died down and it became perfectly calm.

40 And He said to them, "Why are you afraid? Do you still have no faith?"

41 They became very much afraid and said to one another, "Who then is this, that even the wind and the sea obey Him?"

#RemarkableStudy

One parable stacks atop the next. The collection reads like a riddler's handbook of the kingdom of God. Stories of sowers and weeds and mustard seeds flourish throughout Mark 4. Then suddenly, a storm so fierce, the waves break across the bow and threaten to tear apart the hull.

The disciples strain at the oars. They bail water hard and fast. They pray to God. Then they remember God. Is. In. Their. Midst.

Where's Jesus? Enjoying a catnap. Taking a siesta. Nestling in the Land of Nod.

What kind of God snores through a storm? Don't you care that we're drenched and nearly drowned?

"Hush, be still," Jesus whispers to the waves.

Sometimes I wonder who those remarkable words were really spoken toward. The wind went silent and all became still. But Jesus already had all chaos under control.

Perhaps these words were spoken aloud not toward the downpour as much as toward the disciples. Spoken to their fears and tears and doubts and despair. Spoken into their hearts so those words could be spoken into our hearts today.

"Hush, be still," Jesus whispers.

1. What's the biggest storm brewing in your heart?
2. When are you most tempted to doubt God's presence?
3. Where do you most need Jesus to whisper, "Hush, be still"?
4. Using the Color Method, what stood out to you most from today's Scripture?

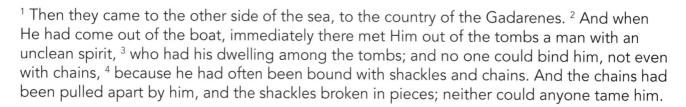

[1] Then they came to the other side of the sea, to the country of the Gadarenes. [2] And when He had come out of the boat, immediately there met Him out of the tombs a man with an unclean spirit, [3] who had his dwelling among the tombs; and no one could bind him, not even with chains, [4] because he had often been bound with shackles and chains. And the chains had been pulled apart by him, and the shackles broken in pieces; neither could anyone tame him.

[5] And always, night and day, he was in the mountains and in the tombs, crying out and cutting himself with stones.

[6] When he saw Jesus from afar, he ran and worshiped Him. [7] And he cried out with a loud voice and said, "What have I to do with You, Jesus, Son of the Most High God? I implore You by God that You do not torment me."

[8] For He said to him, "Come out of the man, unclean spirit!" Then He asked him, "What is your name?" And he answered, saying, "My name is Legion; for we are many." [10] Also he begged Him earnestly that He would not send them out of the country.

[11] Now a large herd of swine was feeding there near the mountains. [12] So all the demons begged Him, saying, "Send us to the swine, that we may enter them."

[13] And at once Jesus gave them permission. Then the unclean spirits went out and entered the swine (there were about two thousand); and the herd ran violently down the steep place into the sea, and drowned in the sea.

[14] So those who fed the swine fled, and they told it in the city and in the country. And they went out to see what it was that had happened. [15] Then they came to Jesus, and saw the one who had been demon-possessed and had the legion, sitting and clothed and in his right mind. And they were afraid.

[16] And those who saw it told them how it happened to him who had been demon-possessed, and about the swine. [17] Then they began to plead with Him to depart from their region.

[18] And when He got into the boat, he who had been demon-possessed begged Him that he might be with Him. [19] However, Jesus did not permit him, but said to him, "Go home to your friends, and tell them what great things the Lord has done for you, and how He has had compassion on you."

[20] And he departed and began to proclaim in Decapolis all that Jesus had done for him; and all marveled.

Imagine muscles so strong, iron chains crumble around you. Yet your grand power makes you a supervillain rather than a superhero. Everyone stays far, far away.

That's the torturous existence of a man whose plague is demons. In darkness, he crawls through the cemetery; in shadows, he retreats to the wild. All the while, he slashes his wrists, his legs, his face. Nothing stops him.

Then Jesus commands. The unclean spirits vanish into unclean animals. The man changes into a clear mind and clean clothes.

As Jesus waves "Bon voyage," the man begs to climb aboard. Who can blame him?

All the shame he's felt from years of unruly behavior. Embarrassed by his actions. Uncertain of social norms. Deep self-consciousness. The temptation to self-blame. No wonder the man tries to make an escape with Jesus.

Yet Jesus says stay. Never allow shame to get the best of you, because God has something remarkable for you. Return to your people with a two-prong mission: tell them (a) the great things the Lord has done for you and (b) how He has had compassion on you.

In the process, we discover a powerful truth:

Your story is a source of God's glory.

1. Describe someone you know whose life has been transformed by Christ.
2. Where do you wrestle with feelings of shame?
3. What would it look like to embrace God's love, compassion, and healing in those areas?
4. Using the Color Method, what stood out to you most from today's Scripture?

21 When Jesus went in the boat back to the other side of the lake, a large crowd gathered around him there. 22 A leader of the synagogue, named Jairus, came there, saw Jesus, and fell at his feet. 23 He begged Jesus, saying again and again, "My daughter is dying. Please come and put your hands on her so she will be healed and will live." 24 So Jesus went with him.

A large crowd followed Jesus and pushed very close around him. 25 Among them was a woman who had been bleeding for twelve years. 26 She had suffered very much from many doctors and had spent all the money she had, but instead of improving, she was getting worse. 27 When the woman heard about Jesus, she came up behind him in the crowd and touched his coat.

28 She thought, "If I can just touch his clothes, I will be healed." 29 Instantly her bleeding stopped, and she felt in her body that she was healed from her disease.

30 At once Jesus felt power go out from him. So he turned around in the crowd and asked, "Who touched my clothes?"

31 His followers said, "Look at how many people are pushing against you! And you ask, 'Who touched me?'"

32 But Jesus continued looking around to see who had touched him. 33 The woman, knowing that she was healed, came and fell at Jesus' feet. Shaking with fear, she told him the whole truth.

34 Jesus said to her, "Dear woman, you are made well because you believed. Go in peace; be healed of your disease."

35 While Jesus was still speaking, some people came from the house of the synagogue leader. They said, "Your daughter is dead. There is no need to bother the teacher anymore."

36 But Jesus paid no attention to what they said. He told the synagogue leader, "Don't be afraid; just believe."

37 Jesus let only Peter, James, and John the brother of James go with him. 38 When they came to the house of the synagogue leader, Jesus found many people there making lots of noise and crying loudly.

39 Jesus entered the house and said to them, "Why are you crying and making so much noise? The child is not dead, only asleep."

⁴⁰ But they laughed at him. So, after throwing them out of the house, Jesus took the child's father and mother and his three followers into the room where the child was. ⁴¹ Taking hold of the girl's hand, he said to her, "Talitha, koum!" (This means, "Young girl, I tell you to stand up!")

⁴² At once the girl stood right up and began walking. (She was twelve years old.) Everyone was completely amazed. ⁴³ Jesus gave them strict orders not to tell people about this. Then he told them to give the girl something to eat.

Jarius throws himself on the ground and begs the Remarkable One to heal his beloved daughter. To Jarius' elation, Jesus agrees, and they make their way to Jarius' house until large crowds block the way.

One woman, desperate for healing, stretches her fingers and brushes against Jesus' cloak. Amid the hustle and bustle, Jesus demands, "Who touched Me?"

The question sounds ridiculous among the throng of humanity. Everyone grasps and grabs, taps and tugs. Yet one woman knows. Like Jarius, she throws herself on the ground. Jesus heals her and sends her off in deep shalom.

With that pinch of delay, Jarius discovers his daughter is dead. Yet Jesus combats death. Soon the young girl's chest fills with air, her heart with rhythm, her father with joy. Jarius has the privilege of watching not one, but two miracles that day, teaching us:

Don't limit God to one miracle when He's working remarkably more.

Sometimes we can be tempted to believe that God will work in someone else's life or ours, yet Jesus is a both/and healer. He works in their life and your life and all lives, all at the same time.

1. What do Jarius and the woman's approaches to Jesus reveal about their faith?
2. What parallels do you see between the two healings? Differences?
3. Where do you need to be reminded of the both/and nature of God?
4. Using the Color Method, what stood out to you most from today's Scripture?

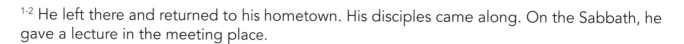

1-2 He left there and returned to his hometown. His disciples came along. On the Sabbath, he gave a lecture in the meeting place.

He made a real hit, impressing everyone. "We had no idea he was this good!" they said. "How did he get so wise all of a sudden, get such ability?"

3 But in the next breath they were cutting him down: "He's just a carpenter—Mary's boy. We've known him since he was a kid. We know his brothers, James, Justus, Jude, and Simon, and his sisters. Who does he think he is?"

They tripped over what little they knew about him and fell, sprawling. And they never got any further.

4-6 Jesus told them, "A prophet has little honor in his hometown, among his relatives, on the streets he played in as a child."

Jesus wasn't able to do much of anything there—he laid hands on a few sick people and healed them, that's all. He couldn't get over their stubbornness. He left and made a circuit of the other villages, teaching.

7-8 Jesus called the Twelve to him, and sent them out in pairs. He gave them authority and power to deal with the evil opposition.

He sent them off with these instructions:

8-9 "Don't think you need a lot of extra equipment for this. You are the equipment. No special appeals for funds. Keep it simple.

10 "And no luxury inns. Get a modest place and be content there until you leave.

11 "If you're not welcomed, not listened to, quietly withdraw. Don't make a scene. Shrug your shoulders and be on your way."

12-13 Then they were on the road.

They preached with joyful urgency that life can be radically different; right and left they sent the demons packing; they brought wellness to the sick, anointing their bodies, healing their spirits.

When Jesus sends the disciples to herald Good News, they aren't even permitted a carry-on. The Gospel of Mark tells us they're sent in pairs, a customary practice in the ancient world. Not only were duos safer, but together they provided validation for their stories (Deuteronomy 17:6).

The Remarkable One instructs His followers-turned-family to travel light. No need to over-prepare. All those duffel bags and handbags and suitcases and backpacks will only weigh you down. Delivering Good News doesn't require extra equipment or fancy gizmos.

No need to bring a flashlight when the Light of the World leads you.
No need to carry pepper spray when the Lord of Armies watches over you.
No need to pack the medicine cabinet when the Great Physician is with you.
No need for a lunch box when the Bread of Life sends you.

You can always travel lighter with God.

Wherever the disciples travel they stay in homes and share joy. The radical message of Jesus delivers freedom, brings healing, and ushers in wholeness.

Not just to those visited by the disciples, but to us, too. Because of their journey, we know we can travel light.

1. In what area of your life are you carrying some extra baggage?
2. Where do you sense God nudging you to walk in greater trust?
3. What steps do you need to take to travel lighter this week?
4. Using the Color Method, what stood out to you most from today's Scripture?

BEFORE YOU SAY ANOTHER WORD
Day 13 - Mark 6:14-32 ESV

14 King Herod heard of it, for Jesus' name had become known. Some said, "John the Baptist has been raised from the dead. That is why these miraculous powers are at work in him."

15 But others said, "He is Elijah." And others said, "He is a prophet, like one of the prophets of old." 16 But when Herod heard of it, he said, "John, whom I beheaded, has been raised."

17 For it was Herod who had sent and seized John and bound him in prison for the sake of Herodias, his brother Philip's wife, because he had married her. 18 For John had been saying to Herod, "It is not lawful for you to have your brother's wife."

19 And Herodias had a grudge against him and wanted to put him to death. But she could not, 20 for Herod feared John, knowing that he was a righteous and holy man, and he kept him safe. When he heard him, he was greatly perplexed, and yet he heard him gladly.

21 But an opportunity came when Herod on his birthday gave a banquet for his nobles and military commanders and the leading men of Galilee. 22 For when Herodias's daughter came in and danced, she pleased Herod and his guests. And the king said to the girl, "Ask me for whatever you wish, and I will give it to you." 23 And he vowed to her, "Whatever you ask me, I will give you, up to half of my kingdom."

24 And she went out and said to her mother, "For what should I ask?" And she said, "The head of John the Baptist." 25 And she came in immediately with haste to the king and asked, saying, "I want you to give me at once the head of John the Baptist on a platter."

26 And the king was exceedingly sorry, but because of his oaths and his guests he did not want to break his word to her. 27 And immediately the king sent an executioner with orders to bring John's head. He went and beheaded him in the prison 28 and brought his head on a platter and gave it to the girl, and the girl gave it to her mother.

29 When his disciples heard of it, they came and took his body and laid it in a tomb.

30 The apostles returned to Jesus and told him all that they had done and taught. 31 And he said to them, "Come away by yourselves to a desolate place and rest a while." For many were coming and going, and they had no leisure even to eat. 32 And they went away in the boat to a desolate place by themselves.

Holy boldness marks John's ministry. The forerunner of Jesus never shrinks back from telling those in power what they least want to hear. He speaks warnings to Herod Antipas, the regional governor. Antipas' father was Herod the Great—the wicked, egotistical ruler who slaughtered countless infants in an effort to eliminate Jesus.

When it comes to this pair of Herods, the apple doesn't fall far from the tree.

Herod Antipas falls in love with his half-brother's wife. John the Baptist tells him he can't be with her. This violates the Torah, the Jewish law. John is perceived as a royal threat and thrown into prison.

One evening, Herod makes a rash and foolish oath, and John's head becomes the main course for an evil plot. The story contains endless insights, but among the most potent: the power of self-discipline.

When it comes to the tongue, some words are better left unsaid.

This isn't true just for ancient kings but for us today as well. I've made mistakes, and I bet you have, too. We cross a line. We speak too soon or say too much. We make a grandiose gesture beyond our means. We say yes before we know the question. We talk before we think.

Through the power of grace, we must rise above the temptation in our deeds and speech. It's never too late to swallow our pride and change direction.

1. Where do you most need to grow in self-control?
2. Describe a situation where your lack of self-discipline harmed someone.
3. In what area are you tempted right now to go against your conscience?
4. Using the Color Method, what stood out to you most from today's Scripture?

33-36 A great many saw them go and recognized them, and people from all the towns hurried around the shore on foot to forestall them.

When Jesus disembarked he saw the large crowd and his heart was touched with pity for them because they seemed to him like sheep without a shepherd.

And he settled down to teach them about many things.

As the day wore on, his disciples came to him and said, "We are right in the wilds here and it is getting late.

Let them go now, so that they can buy themselves something to eat from the farms and villages around here"

37 But Jesus replied, "You give them something to eat!"

"You mean we're to go and spend ten pounds on bread (equivalent to six month's wages)? Is that how you want us to feed them?"

38 "What bread have you got?" asked Jesus. "Go and have a look."

And when they found out, they told him, "We have five loaves and two fish."

39-44 Then Jesus directed the people to sit down in parties on the fresh grass. And they threw themselves down in groups of fifty and a hundred.

Then Jesus took the five loaves and the two fish, and looking up to Heaven, thanked God, broke the loaves and gave them to the disciples to distribute to the people.

And he divided the two fish among them all.

Everybody ate and was satisfied.

Afterwards they collected twelve baskets full of pieces of bread and fish that were left over.

There were five thousand men who ate the loaves.

In John's account of this story, Jesus and the followers-turned-family climb a mountain on the far side of the Sea of Galilee. Throngs of people soon surround Jesus and hang on His every word. Jesus teaches until the sun flirts with the horizon. The disciples become concerned for low blood sugar throughout the crowd.

Jesus instructs the disciples to feed the masses. His followers crunch numbers and realize the cost is prohibitive. The Remarkable One has a plan, but waits to deepen the disciples' faith.

A boy donates his lunch. The small portion appears insignificant. Yet Jesus accepts the child's offering and requests everyone take a seat. The people nest on the grass, eager to see what Jesus will do next.

One can imagine the seed of doubt in the disciples' hearts as they look at the loaves and fish. But Jesus doesn't hesitate. He takes the bread and gives thanks over the meal. The food is distributed and the meal multiplies before the disciples' eyes.

Distracted by the wow-factor of this remarkable miracle, the crowd doesn't realize Jesus isn't concerned just with their physical hunger but with their spiritual hunger. This miracle isn't about multiplying loaves as much as revealing Christ as the Messiah—their long-awaited Savior.

When you're looking for a short-term fix, remember God aims for long-term transformation.

Sometimes when we find ourselves in great need, we can become so focused on the provision, we forget the Provider. No matter what you're facing right now, rest assured God's provision includes not just a solution but a superabundance of His presence.

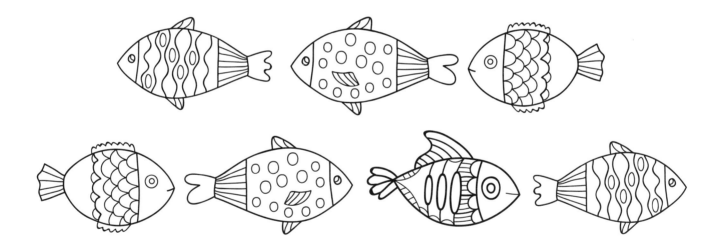

1. When was a time you disqualified yourself because your offering seemed inadequate?

2. Which of your prayer requests focuses on short-term fixes?

3. In what specific areas do you suspect God is aiming for long-term transformation?

4. Using the Color Method, what stood out to you most from today's Scripture?

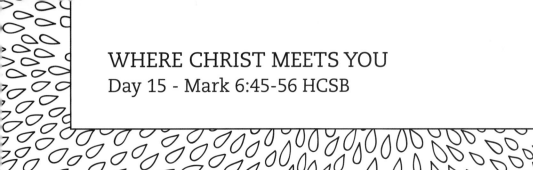

⁴⁵ Immediately He made His disciples get into the boat and go ahead of Him to the other side, to Bethsaida, while He dismissed the crowd. ⁴⁶ After He said good-bye to them, He went away to the mountain to pray. ⁴⁷ When evening came, the boat was in the middle of the sea, and He was alone on the land. ⁴⁸ He saw them being battered as they rowed, because the wind was against them. Around three in the morning He came toward them walking on the sea and wanted to pass by them.

⁴⁹ When they saw Him walking on the sea, they thought it was a ghost and cried out; ⁵⁰ for they all saw Him and were terrified. Immediately He spoke with them and said, "Have courage! It is I. Don't be afraid." ⁵¹ Then He got into the boat with them, and the wind ceased. They were completely astounded, ⁵² because they had not understood about the loaves. Instead, their hearts were hardened.

⁵³ When they had crossed over, they came to land at Gennesaret and beached the boat. ⁵⁴ As they got out of the boat, people immediately recognized Him. ⁵⁵ They hurried throughout that vicinity and began to carry the sick on mats to wherever they heard He was. ⁵⁶ Wherever He would go, into villages, towns, or the country, they laid the sick in the marketplaces and begged Him that they might touch just the tassel of His robe. And everyone who touched it was made well.

Many of my friends have what I call "The Star Trek Calling." They go where others have not gone before. They cross borders. Push boundaries. Explore uncharted frontiers. All because God nudges them.

Perhaps I'm describing you.

Those with "The Star Trek Calling" travel to places in time and space where others are slow to venture.

Sometimes these friends move forward on a holy nudge, a sacred whim, an unshakable prodding. They develop programs, nonprofits, foundations, blogs, books, outreaches. They love their neighbors, raise children to follow Jesus, and transform schools and workplaces. They follow obediently, disrupting the status quo of pain and poverty, faithlessness and darkness, abuse and exploitation.

But they also encounter hardship, loss, and storms. Much like the disciples caught in a wicked storm, they second-guess if they'll make it, if they have what it takes, if God will rescue them.

Yet the story of the disciples crossing a chaotic expanse teaches:

Christ wants to meet you in the middle of the mess.

Jesus isn't waiting until you get to the other side, finish the project, complete the task. The Remarkable One who nudged you, called you, and sent you remains with you. And there's no storm that you'll face that Jesus can't overcome.

Take courage, all you trekkers with Jesus: He is with you every step of the way. Live long and prosper in His loving presence. That's really good news.

1. What is one impossible task to which God has called you?
2. How has Christ met you in the middle of your mess?
3. How have you experienced God's grace in your weakness?
4. Using the Color Method, what stood out to you most from today's Scripture?

[1] The Pharisees and some of the scribes gathered around Him when they had come from Jerusalem, [2] and had seen that some of His disciples were eating their bread with impure hands, that is, unwashed. [3] (For the Pharisees and all the Jews do not eat unless they carefully wash their hands, thus observing the traditions of the elders; [4] and when they come from the market place, they do not eat unless they cleanse themselves; and there are many other things which they have received in order to observe, such as the washing of cups and pitchers and copper pots.)

[5] The Pharisees and the scribes asked Him, "Why do Your disciples not walk according to the tradition of the elders, but eat their bread with impure hands?" [6] And He said to them, "Rightly did Isaiah prophesy of you hypocrites, as it is written: 'This people honors Me with their lips, But their heart is far away from Me. [7] 'But in vain do they worship Me, Teaching as doctrines the precepts of men.' [8] Neglecting the commandment of God, you hold to the tradition of men."

[9] He was also saying to them, "You are experts at setting aside the commandment of God in order to keep your tradition. [10] For Moses said, 'Honor your father and your mother'; and, 'He who speaks evil of father or mother, is to be put to death'; [11] but you say, 'If a man says to his father or his mother, whatever I have that would help you is Corban (that is to say, given to God),' [12] you no longer permit him to do anything for his father or his mother; [13] thus invalidating the word of God by your tradition which you have handed down; and you do many things such as that."

[14] After He called the crowd to Him again, He began saying to them, "Listen to Me, all of you, and understand: [15] there is nothing outside the man which can defile him if it goes into him; but the things which proceed out of the man are what defile the man. [16] [If anyone has ears to hear, let him hear."]

[17] When he had left the crowd and entered the house, His disciples questioned Him about the parable. [18] And He said to them, "Are you so lacking in understanding also? Do you not understand that whatever goes into the man from outside cannot defile him, [19] because it does not go into his heart, but into his stomach, and is eliminated?" (Thus He declared all foods clean.) [20] And He was saying, "That which proceeds out of the man, that is what defiles the man. [21] For from within, out of the heart of men, proceed the evil thoughts, fornications, thefts, murders, adulteries, [22] deeds of coveting and wickedness, as well as deceit, sensuality, envy, slander, pride and foolishness. [23] All these evil things proceed from within and defile the man."

Jesus lives under a microscope. The Pharisees and the teachers of the law scout every minute detail to accuse Jesus. Throughout the Gospel of Mark, the religious leaders rubberneck to catch Jesus making a mistake. Yet Jesus reminds His disciples that the kingdom of God doesn't expand through the work of religious paparazzi.

Perhaps that's one reason Jesus goes on to tell us that things aren't as they appear. The great law isn't judgment but love.

Love deep. Love hard. Love anyway.

Apart from love, religious laws become life-choking legalism. Through legalism things appear shiny on the outside but remain septic on the inside.

Why is legalism so toxic?

Legalism builds towering walls no one can climb. Legalism barricades people out. Legalism cuts us off from others, including their story and their gifts. Legalism diminishes our opportunity to learn, grow, and mature.

The heavy cost of legalism is that you don't just cut yourself off from others, you cut yourself off from the remarkable, redemptive work God is doing in people's lives.

1. When have you been hurt by someone's legalism?
2. When have you hurt others through legalistic beliefs?
3. Where are you currently struggling with legalism?
4. Using the Color Method, what stood out to you most from today's Scripture?

²⁴ Jesus got up and went away from there to the region of Tyre. And when He had entered a house, He wanted no one to know of it; yet He could not escape notice.

²⁵ But after hearing of Him, a woman whose little daughter had an unclean spirit immediately came and fell at His feet.

²⁶ Now the woman was a Gentile, of the Syrophoenician race. And she kept asking Him to cast the demon out of her daughter.

²⁷ And He was saying to her, "Let the children be satisfied first, for it is not good to take the children's bread and throw it to the dogs."

²⁸ But she answered and said to Him, "Yes, Lord, but even the dogs under the table feed on the children's crumbs." ²⁹ And He said to her, "Because of this answer go; the demon has gone out of your daughter."

³⁰ And going back to her home, she found the child lying on the bed, the demon having left.

³¹ Again He went out from the region of Tyre, and came through Sidon to the Sea of Galilee, within the region of Decapolis.

³² They brought to Him one who was deaf and spoke with difficulty, and they implored Him to lay His hand on him.

³³ Jesus took him aside from the crowd, by himself, and put His fingers into his ears, and after spitting, He touched his tongue with the saliva;

³⁴ and looking up to heaven with a deep sigh, He said to him, "Ephphatha!" that is, "Be opened!"

³⁵ And his ears were opened, and the impediment of his tongue was removed, and he began speaking plainly.

³⁶ And He gave them orders not to tell anyone; but the more He ordered them, the more widely they continued to proclaim it.

³⁷ They were utterly astonished, saying, "He has done all things well; He makes even the deaf to hear and the mute to speak."

One remarkable word zaps from the page: *kept.*

Perhaps you missed the small, unassuming syllable that explodes with holy chutzpah and dogged determination. A Syrophoenician woman bats away social norms and expectations. With a shrill cry, she pleads for Christ's pity. Will the Remarkable One heal her daughter who's been terrorized by a dark spirit?

That's where the word kept appears (vs. 26). She kept asking. *Kept* pursuing. *Kept* pleading. *Kept* trusting. *Kept* hounding. *Kept* chasing. Jesus brushes her off like crumbs from a table. He has only come for the lost sheep of Israel. Even the mongrels survive on the table droppings, she rebuts. With that answer, her daughter is cured.

She kept on.

But it's not just her. In the follow-up story, some people *implore* Jesus to heal their deaf friend. That's more than a request—more like a passionate begging. He's healed, too.

Both the woman and the friends of the deaf man exhibit a holy chutzpah, a dogged determination. Together, they remind us:

As followers of Jesus, we must keep on keeping on.

When it comes to trusting God through prayer, never give up.

1. In what area of your life have you lost your holy tenacity?
2. Why have you stopped asking God with persistent prayer?
3. Write a prayer of holy chutzpah, a bold request, to God.
4. Using the Color Method, what stood out to you most from today's Scripture?

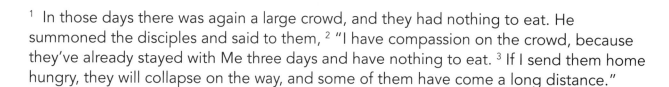

¹ In those days there was again a large crowd, and they had nothing to eat. He summoned the disciples and said to them, ² "I have compassion on the crowd, because they've already stayed with Me three days and have nothing to eat. ³ If I send them home hungry, they will collapse on the way, and some of them have come a long distance."

⁴ His disciples answered Him, "Where can anyone get enough bread here in this desolate place to fill these people?" ⁵ "How many loaves do you have?" He asked them. "Seven," they said.

⁶ Then He commanded the crowd to sit down on the ground. Taking the seven loaves, He gave thanks, broke the loaves, and kept on giving them to His disciples to set before the people. So they served the loaves to the crowd.

⁷ They also had a few small fish, and when He had blessed them, He said these were to be served as well. ⁸ They ate and were filled. Then they collected seven large baskets of leftover pieces. ⁹ About 4,000 men were there. He dismissed them ¹⁰ and immediately got into the boat with His disciples and went to the district of Dalmanutha.

¹¹ The Pharisees came out and began to argue with Him, demanding of Him a sign from heaven to test Him. ¹² But sighing deeply in His spirit, He said, "Why does this generation demand a sign? I assure you: No sign will be given to this generation!" ¹³ Then He left them, got on board the boat again, and went to the other side.

¹⁴ They had forgotten to take bread and had only one loaf with them in the boat. ¹⁵ Then He commanded them: "Watch out! Beware of the yeast of the Pharisees and the yeast of Herod."

¹⁶ They were discussing among themselves that they did not have any bread. ¹⁷ Aware of this, He said to them, "Why are you discussing that you do not have any bread? Don't you understand or comprehend? Is your heart hardened? ¹⁸ Do you have eyes, and not see, and do you have ears, and not hear? And do you not remember? ¹⁹ When I broke the five loaves for the 5,000, how many baskets full of pieces of bread did you collect?" "Twelve," they told Him.

²⁰ "When I broke the seven loaves for the 4,000, how many large baskets full of pieces of bread did you collect?" "Seven," they said.

²¹ And He said to them, "Don't you understand yet?"

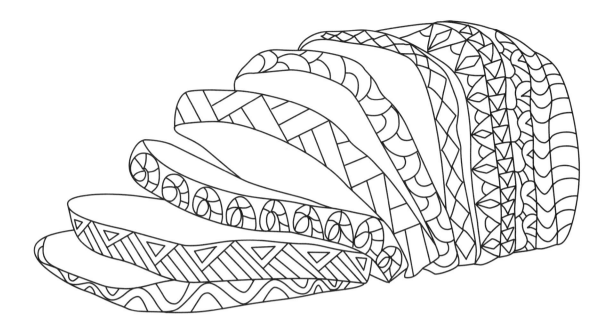

The disciples already stood in awe when Jesus opened up shop—a bakery and fish factory—for thousands, using only a blessing and a boy's lunchbox. Now we find ourselves here *again*. Surrounded by hungry crowds *again*.

Some scholars believe this second account is an accidental repetition. Yet this is a feast and a miracle deserves more than a second glance because…

God alone bakes up hearty satisfaction.

Like the first account, the divine (not the devil) is in the details.

Jesus reminds the disciples He's been with the people for three days. The writer of Mark wants us to understand the passion of Christ. In three days, His body will rise (Mark 8:31, 9:31, 10:34) and a new temple emerge (Mark 15:29). The number three helps us understand the death and resurrection of Christ in the context of a meal. The table is open to both Jews and Gentiles, women and children.

Instead of five loaves and two fish, seven large loaves emerge, the perfect number.

And instead of gathering 12 regular baskets in the first meal, they now gather seven very large baskets. The Greek word is *spuris*, a human-sized hamper—the same word used when Paul is lowered from a high window in Acts 9:25. This is a remarkable story of superabundance.

The Bread of Life proclaims through a powerful deed that all who feast on Him will forever be satisfied.

1. In what specific ways has Christ filled you with superabundance?
2. Who are you most tempted to exclude from your table?
3. How has using the Color Method helped you notice details from Scripture?
4. Using the Color Method, what stood out to you most from today's Scripture?

22 They came to Bethsaida, and some people brought a blind man and begged Jesus to touch him. 23 He took the blind man by the hand and led him outside the village. When he had spit on the man's eyes and put his hands on him, Jesus asked, "Do you see anything?"

24 He looked up and said, "I see people; they look like trees walking around."

25 Once more Jesus put his hands on the man's eyes. Then his eyes were opened, his sight was restored, and he saw everything clearly. 26 Jesus sent him home, saying, "Don't even go into the village."

27 Jesus and his disciples went on to the villages around Caesarea Philippi. On the way he asked them, "Who do people say I am?"

28 They replied, "Some say John the Baptist; others say Elijah; and still others, one of the prophets."

29 "But what about you?" he asked. "Who do you say I am?" Peter answered, "You are the Messiah."

30 Jesus warned them not to tell anyone about him.

31 He then began to teach them that the Son of Man must suffer many things and be rejected by the elders, the chief priests and the teachers of the law, and that he must be killed and after three days rise again. 32 He spoke plainly about this, and Peter took him aside and began to rebuke him.

33 But when Jesus turned and looked at his disciples, he rebuked Peter. "Get behind me, Satan!" he said. "You do not have in mind the concerns of God, but merely human concerns."

34 Then he called the crowd to him along with his disciples and said: "Whoever wants to be my disciple must deny themselves and take up their cross and follow me. 35 For whoever wants to save their life will lose it, but whoever loses their life for me and for the gospel will save it. 36 What good is it for someone to gain the whole world, yet forfeit their soul? 37 Or what can anyone give in exchange for their soul?

38 If anyone is ashamed of me and my words in this adulterous and sinful generation, the Son of Man will be ashamed of them when he comes in his Father's glory with the holy angels."

Rocks rumble and tumble with rolling waves along the seashore. They skip when tossed across the surface of the water. They also sink, hard and fast. Rocks can be used to build up and to throw down. Giants have even been toppled by them. A solid rock can become a cornerstone.

Perhaps Jesus had all these images in mind when He dubbed Simon His little "Rocky" and began calling him Peter. In Mark 8, we catch a glimpse of just how fast a rock, like Peter, can roll. "Who do people say I am?" Jesus asks.

The disciples burst with answers like popcorn. John the Immerser. Elijah. Another fill-in-the-blank prophet of old. Jesus cracks a slight grin. Jesus now turns to those closest to Him.

"Who do you say I am?" Jesus asks.

Little Rocky tosses himself into the ring. "You are the Messiah," Peter proclaims. A hush falls on everyone who hears the declaration—even today.

The writer of Mark's Gospel juxtaposes Peter's bold declaration against his folly.

Jesus transitions from the famed question, "Who do you say I am?" to whisper of the suffering and slaughter to come. The religious leaders will reject Him. The teachers of the law will plead for an execution. The mobs will shout for His death. Peter can't bear Jesus' words. They're too dark, too heavy, too much. Peter pulls his Messiah aside to talk Him down, to tug the Son of God from His madness.

"Get behind me, Satan!" Jesus rebukes. "You don't have in mind the concerns of God, but merely human concerns."

The rock rolls in the wrong direction. Mark's placement of these episodes of Jesus' little Rocky, reminds us that proclaiming Jesus as the Messiah is only the first step to becoming a true follower. Then, hour by hour and inch by inch, we must give up our image, our expectations of what we think the Messiah will do and be for us, to embrace who He really is and where He's really taking us.

As followers of Jesus, we are all cross-bound.

May you have the great grace today to pick up those wooden beams and follow wherever the Remarkable One may lead.

1. When have your expectations of God led you to disappointment?
2. Where are you being challenged to pick up your cross in obedience?
3. How have you experienced obedience leading to God's glory?
4. Using the Color Method, what stood out to you most from today's Scripture?

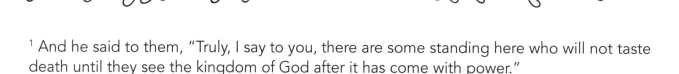
¹ And he said to them, "Truly, I say to you, there are some standing here who will not taste death until they see the kingdom of God after it has come with power."

² And after six days Jesus took with him Peter and James and John, and led them up a high mountain by themselves. And he was transfigured before them, ³ and his clothes became radiant, intensely white, as no one on earth could bleach them.⁴ And there appeared to them Elijah with Moses, and they were talking with Jesus.

⁵ And Peter said to Jesus, "Rabbi, it is good that we are here. Let us make three tents, one for you and one for Moses and one for Elijah." ⁶ For he did not know what to say, for they were terrified.

⁷ And a cloud overshadowed them, and a voice came out of the cloud, "This is my beloved Son; listen to him." ⁸ And suddenly, looking around, they no longer saw anyone with them but Jesus only.

⁹ And as they were coming down the mountain, he charged them to tell no one what they had seen, until the Son of Man had risen from the dead. ¹⁰ So they kept the matter to themselves, questioning what this rising from the dead might mean.¹¹ And they asked him, "Why do the scribes say that first Elijah must come?"

¹² And he said to them, "Elijah does come first to restore all things. And how is it written of the Son of Man that he should suffer many things and be treated with contempt? ¹³ But I tell you that Elijah has come, and they did to him whatever they pleased, as it is written of him."

In a holy moment, the Old Testament smashes into the New. Prophets of the past encounter the followers of the future on a rocky mountainside. Moses. Elijah. James. John. Peter. Jesus. A holy voice echoes a familiar refrain: "This is my beloved Son: Listen to him."

Remarkable syllables spoken for saints of old and for us today. Words for relishing. Christ speaks, and we are invited, welcomed, chosen, called to listen. Yet much stands in the way. Chores. Duties. Tasks. Expectations. Goals. White noise. Loud noise. We ache for the words that heal, the words that restore; yet "First let me _____" slows our resolve. We'll listen later.

Later has a way of making us dilly-dally.
Later has a way of making us unresponsive.
Later has a way of making us disobedient.

I've told God "Later" far too many times. Maybe you have, too. Together let us pray:

Help us be quick to hear, quick to respond, quick to obey.

My prayer for you today is that you recognize God's sacred echoes and walk in the fullness of all God has for you, not later but today.

1. What tends to distract or deafen you from listening to God?
2. When have you sensed the Lord speaking to you lately?
3. What's one of the most meaningful echoes God has ever spoken to you?
4. Using the Color Method, what stood out to you most from today's Scripture?

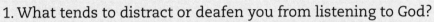

WHAT IF YOU'RE MEASURING THINGS ALL WRONG?
Day 21 - Mark 9:14-29 NRSV

14 And when they came to the disciples, they saw a great crowd about them, and scribes arguing with them. 15 And immediately all the crowd, when they saw him, were greatly amazed, and ran up to him and greeted him. 16 And he asked them, "What are you discussing with them?"

17 And one of the crowd answered him, "Teacher, I brought my son to you, for he has a dumb spirit; 18 and wherever it seizes him, it dashes him down; and he foams and grinds his teeth and becomes rigid; and I asked your disciples to cast it out, and they were not able."

19 And he answered them, "O faithless generation, how long am I to be with you? How long am I to bear with you? Bring him to me." 20 And they brought the boy to him; and when the spirit saw him, immediately it convulsed the boy, and he fell on the ground and rolled about, foaming at the mouth.

21 And Jesus asked his father, "How long has he had this?" And he said, "From childhood. 22 And it has often cast him into the fire and into the water, to destroy him; but if you can do anything, have pity on us and help us." 23 And Jesus said to him, "If you can! All things are possible to him who believes."

24 Immediately the father of the child cried out and said, "I believe; help my unbelief!" 25 And when Jesus saw that a crowd came running together, he rebuked the unclean spirit, saying to it, "You dumb and deaf spirit, I command you, come out of him, and never enter him again." 26 And after crying out and convulsing him terribly, it came out, and the boy was like a corpse; so that most of them said, "He is dead."

27 But Jesus took him by the hand and lifted him up, and he arose. 28 And when he had entered the house, his disciples asked him privately, "Why could we not cast it out?" 29 And he said to them, "This kind cannot be driven out by anything but prayer."

Three disciples venture with Jesus to the transfiguration and touch heaven. Nine remain behind to wrestle with hell. A young boy tortured by evil spirits needs freedom, but the disciples have none to give. Jesus proclaims in frustration, "O faithless generation." Then Jesus engages in a playful dialogue with the father.

The father says, "if you can." Jesus responds, "If you can! All things are possible to him who believes." Jesus knows the man has faith or else he wouldn't have brought his son for healing. The father cries out, "I believe; help my unbelief!"

How much faith did the father have? A ton, 100 kilos, an ounce, or a milligram? We don't know. But in the midst of a "faithless generation," his was enough.

Sometimes it's tempting to measure the weight of our faith. Do we have enough pounds or kilos or energy or enthusiasm? Yet God never approaches us with a scale in hand. Whenever we try to measure our faith, we measure all wrong. Why?

Instead of measuring your faith, God multiplies it.

No matter how much or how little faith you have today, you can offer it to God and ask Him to give you what you do not have. Through prayer, you can join the father in crying out, "I believe; help my unbelief!"

1. When are you tempted to believe you don't measure up in faith?
2. Where are you most confident in your faith right now?
3. Where are you struggling with unbelief most?
4. Using the Color Method, what stood out to you most from today's Scripture?

YOU CAN ASK THIS ANYTIME
Day 22 - Mark 9:30-50 NKJV

30 Then they departed from there and passed through Galilee, and He did not want anyone to know it. 31 For He taught His disciples and said to them, "The Son of Man is being betrayed into the hands of men, and they will kill Him. And after He is killed, He will rise the third day." 32 But they did not understand this saying, and were afraid to ask Him.

33 Then He came to Capernaum. And when He was in the house He asked them, "What was it you disputed among yourselves on the road?" 34 But they kept silent, for on the road they had disputed among themselves who would be the greatest. 35 And He sat down, called the twelve, and said to them, "If anyone desires to be first, he shall be last of all and servant of all."

36 Then He took a little child and set him in the midst of them. And when He had taken him in His arms, He said to them, 37 "Whoever receives one of these little children in My name receives Me; and whoever receives Me, receives not Me but Him who sent Me."

38 Now John answered Him, saying, "Teacher, we saw someone who does not follow us casting out demons in Your name, and we forbade him because he does not follow us."

39 But Jesus said, "Do not forbid him, for no one who works a miracle in My name can soon afterward speak evil of Me. 40 For he who is not against us is on our side. 41 For whoever gives you a cup of water to drink in My name, because you belong to Christ, assuredly, I say to you, he will by no means lose his reward.

42 "But whoever causes one of these little ones who believe in Me to stumble, it would be better for him if a millstone were hung around his neck, and he were thrown into the sea. 43 If your hand causes you to sin, cut it off. It is better for you to enter into life maimed, rather than having two hands, to go to hell, into the fire that shall never be quenched— 44 where 'Their worm does not die and the fire is not quenched.' 45 And if your foot causes you to sin, cut it off. It is better for you to enter life lame, rather than having two feet, to be cast into hell, into the fire that shall never be quenched— 46 where 'Their worm does not die, and the fire is not quenched.'

47 And if your eye causes you to sin, pluck it out. It is better for you to enter the kingdom of God with one eye, rather than having two eyes, to be cast into hell fire— 48 where 'Their worm does not die and the fire is not quenched.'

49 "For everyone will be seasoned with fire, and every sacrifice will be seasoned with salt. 50Salt *is* good, but if the salt loses its flavor, how will you season it? Have salt in yourselves, and have peace with one another."

The Remarkable One predicts His death and resurrection. This isn't the first time. Jesus has warned His disciples before the rejection by chief priests, Jewish elders, and scribes (Mark 8:31). The Son of God is destined for great suffering.

In Galilee, Jesus echoes again that He will be betrayed and killed. After three days, He will rise again. Yet the disciples still don't understand, and "they were afraid to ask him" (Mark 9:32).

Next, the disciples debate their ratings as if following Jesus is a reality show competition. Instead of gazing at Christ's greatness, they reflect on their own. Jesus realigns their thinking by bouncing a child on His knee.

Reflecting on this passage, I can't help but wonder if the story would have a different ending if they'd simply not been afraid to ask Jesus their questions. Perhaps they would have avoided the who's-the-greatest-discussion-altogether. Perhaps their focus would have remained on Christ instead of themselves. We'll never know. But rest assured:

No question is too scary for God.

In the moments you're perplexed and confused, don't hesitate to ask God your tough questions, confess your deep doubts, or ask for clarification. There's no need to be afraid.

1. What questions are you least likely to ask God?
2. If you could ask God anything, what would you ask? Ask Him now.
3. When have you asked God a question and received an answer that changed you?
4. Using the Color Method, what stood out to you most from today's Scripture?

THE TRUTH ABOUT LOOPHOLES
Day 23 - Mark 10:1-12 MSG

1-2 From there he went to the area of Judea across the Jordan. A crowd of people, as was so often the case, went along, and he, as he so often did, taught them. Pharisees came up, intending to give him a hard time. They asked, "Is it legal for a man to divorce his wife?"

3 Jesus said, "What did Moses command?"

⁴ They answered, "Moses gave permission to fill out a certificate of dismissal and divorce her."
⁵⁻⁹ Jesus said, "Moses wrote this command only as a concession to your hardhearted ways. In the original creation, God made male and female to be together. Because of this, a man leaves father and mother, and in marriage he becomes one flesh with a woman—no longer two individuals, but forming a new unity. Because God created this organic union of the two sexes, no one should desecrate his art by cutting them apart."

¹⁰⁻¹² When they were back home, the disciples brought it up again. Jesus gave it to them straight: "A man who divorces his wife so he can marry someone else commits adultery against her. And a woman who divorces her husband so she can marry someone else commits adultery."

Where Jesus goes, the crowds smoosh in and the religious leaders follow in tow. A multitude of intentions press together. Some come to learn, others to gawk. Some seek healing, others understanding. Some are curious, others oblivious.

Whenever the religious leaders ask a question, it's almost always for the purpose of watching Jesus trip, tumble, stumble, or fumble. This time they raise the painful question of divorce. One can only imagine the women, deserted by their husbands and left impoverished, who lean in extra close to hear Jesus' response.

The Pharisees look to see if Jesus will affirm those who skirt the law or those who follow it to a T. Yet Jesus points them (and us) to a greater law: the remarkable law of love. In the process, Jesus teaches a heavenly principle:

Love trumps loopholes.

All of us will face the temptation to either evade the law with crafty tactics or leverage the law to fulfill our own desires. Yet neither the law nor its loopholes will save us. Only Christ can.

Rather than search the Scripture for the exceptions, look for the Exceptional One who calls you to greater depths of love than you've ever known before.

1. Do you tend to expect the law to save you or find loopholes around the law? Explain.
2. When have you trusted a loophole but later discovered love is the better way?
3. When have you trusted the law but later discovered love is the better way?
4. Using the Color Method, what stood out to you most from today's Scripture?

13 Some people were bringing little children to Him so He might touch them, but His disciples rebuked them. 14 When Jesus saw it, He was indignant and said to them, "Let the little children come to Me. Don't stop them, for the kingdom of God belongs to such as these. 15 I assure you: Whoever does not welcome the kingdom of God like a little child will never enter it." 16 After taking them in His arms, He laid His hands on them and blessed them.

17 As He was setting out on a journey, a man ran up, knelt down before Him, and asked Him, "Good Teacher, what must I do to inherit eternal life?"

18 "Why do you call Me good?" Jesus asked him. "No one is good but One—God. 19 You know the commandments: Do not murder; do not commit adultery; do not steal; do not bear false witness; do not defraud; honor your father and mother."

20 He said to Him, "Teacher, I have kept all these from my youth."

21 Then, looking at him, Jesus loved him and said to him, "You lack one thing: Go, sell all you have and give to the poor, and you will have treasure in heaven. Then come, follow Me." 22 But he was stunned at this demand, and he went away grieving, because he had many possessions.

23 Jesus looked around and said to His disciples, "How hard it is for those who have wealth to enter the kingdom of God!" 24 But the disciples were astonished at His words. Again Jesus said to them, "Children, how hard it is to enter the kingdom of God! 25 It is easier for a camel to go through the eye of a needle than for a rich person to enter the kingdom of God."

26 So they were even more astonished, saying to one another, "Then who can be saved?" 27 Looking at them, Jesus said, "With men it is impossible, but not with God, because all things are possible with God."

28 Peter began to tell Him, "Look, we have left everything and followed You."

29 "I assure you," Jesus said, "there is no one who has left house, brothers or sisters, mother or father, children, or fields because of Me and the gospel, 30 who will not receive 100 times more, now at this time—houses, brothers and sisters, mothers and children, and fields, with persecutions—and eternal life in the age to come. 31 But many who are first will be last, and the last first."

The kingdom of God turns everything upside down in Mark 10. The Pharisees try to wrap their heads around the question of *how* the kingdom functions as they inquire about divorce. The disciples discover they don't understand the question of *who* the kingdom of God is for when they shoo away toddlers. A trustafarian attempts to understand *what* the kingdom requires of him and grieves Jesus' response. Jesus teaches *why* the kingdom of God is so hard to enter when you're weighed down with material concerns.

Little Rocky furrows his brows, "Look, we have left everything and followed You" (Mark 10:28).

Cut to the core, bare bones, stripped down, Rocky asks: *What's in it for me?*

This question resides deep within the recesses of the hearts of Jesus followers everywhere. We rarely say these aloud, let alone as straightforward as Rocky.

When tough circumstances thwart our lives, our bank accounts, our professions, our families, our futures, we pause and wonder: *What's in it for me?*

The truth is that following Jesus doesn't make us richer, thinner, smarter, or more famous. That can be hard to swallow, especially if someone tricked us early on with false promises and untrue premises. The Remarkable One we follow was filleted open and nailed to a tree. Why would we think it would be different for you or me? Yet Jesus affirms:

When we give up our all for God's all, we get it all.

1. When have you asked God "What's in it for me?"
2. When have you experienced something that made it harder to trust God?
3. What do you sense God asking you to give up to get more of Him?
4. Using the Color Method, what stood out to you most from today's Scripture?

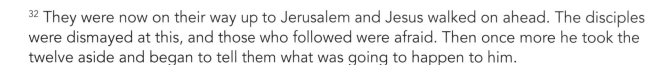
32 They were now on their way up to Jerusalem and Jesus walked on ahead. The disciples were dismayed at this, and those who followed were afraid. Then once more he took the twelve aside and began to tell them what was going to happen to him.

33-34 "We are now going up to Jerusalem," he said, "as you can see. And the Son of Man will be betrayed into the power of the chief priests and scribes. They are going to condemn him to death and hand him over to pagans who will jeer at him and spit at him and flog him and kill him. But after three days he will rise again."

35 Then Zebedee's two sons James and John approached him, saying "Master, we want you to grant us a special request." 36 "What do you want me to do for you?" answered Jesus.
37 "Give us permission to sit one on each side of you in the glory of your kingdom!"

38 "You don't know what you are asking," Jesus said to them. "Can you drink the cup I have to drink? Can you go through the baptism I have to bear?"

39-40 "Yes, we can," they replied. Then Jesus told them, "You will indeed drink the cup I am drinking, and you will undergo the baptism which I have to bear! But as for sitting on either side of me, that is not for me to give—such places belong to those for whom they are intended."

41-45 When the other ten heard about this, they began to be highly indignant with James and John; so Jesus called them all to him, and said, "You know that the so-called rulers in the heathen world lord it over them, and their great men have absolute power. But it must not be so among you. No, whoever among you wants to be great must become the servant of you all, and if he wants to be first among you he must be the slave of all men! For the Son of Man himself has not come to be served but to serve, and to give his life to set many others free."

46-47 Then they came to Jericho, and as he was leaving it accompanied by his disciples and a large crowd, Bartimeus (that is, the son of Timaeus), a blind beggar, was sitting in his usual place by the side of the road. When he heard that it was Jesus of Nazareth he began to call out, "Jesus, Son of David, have pity on me!"

48 Many of the people told him sharply to keep quiet, but he shouted all the more, "Son of David, have pity on me!"

49 Jesus stood quite still and said, "Call him here." So they called the blind man, saying,

"It's all right now, get up, he's calling you!" [50] At this he threw off his coat, jumped to his feet and came to Jesus.

[51] "What do you want me to do for you?" he asked him. "Oh, Master, let me see again!"

[52] "Go on your way then," returned Jesus, "your faith has healed you." And he recovered his sight at once and followed Jesus along the road.

When was the last time you opened your Facebook or Instagram account and felt a pinch of envy? Or drove by the gates of that fancy neighborhood and thought, "Must be nice"? Or looked at someone and felt annoyed that they always seem to have the perfect life?

Sometimes it can seem like everyone else has a better house, a newer car, a dreamier boyfriend, a stronger marriage, an easier time with pregnancy, better-behaved kids or grandkids, less debt, more income, an easier transition to empty-nesting, a larger retirement account, smaller worries, fewer concerns, a better life.

If you're human, sooner or later, you'll experience the twinges of the jaded eye.

The disciples too slip into comparison and jealousy. Today's reading reminds us of Mark 9:30-50 (Day 22). *Again* Jesus predicts His sufferings. *Again* the disciples compete, this time for best placement.

The Thunder Brothers, James and John, elbow their way toward the top leaving the rest of the disciples indignant, resentful, livid. That's what comparison and jealousy do best—leave us frustrated, empty, and discontent. Jesus whispers a better way to live:

Lead by serving and live by dying.

Then, Jesus embodies His teaching, and we discover that the key to winning is not through accomplishment and accolades but through loving and serving others.

1. What situations cause you to fall into the comparison trap?
2. Instead of climbing higher, where do you need to reach lower?
3. Describe a time when serving others sparked great joy in your life?
4. Using the Color Method, what stood out to you most from today's Scripture?

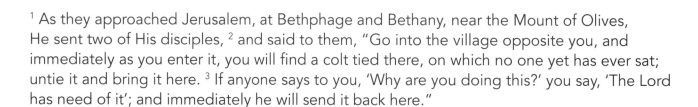

¹ As they approached Jerusalem, at Bethphage and Bethany, near the Mount of Olives, He sent two of His disciples, ² and said to them, "Go into the village opposite you, and immediately as you enter it, you will find a colt tied there, on which no one yet has ever sat; untie it and bring it here. ³ If anyone says to you, 'Why are you doing this?' you say, 'The Lord has need of it'; and immediately he will send it back here."

⁴ They went away and found a colt tied at the door, outside in the street; and they untied it. ⁵ Some of the bystanders were saying to them, "What are you doing, untying the colt?" ⁶ They spoke to them just as Jesus had told them, and they gave them permission. ⁷ They brought the colt to Jesus and put their coats on it; and He sat on it. ⁸ And many spread their coats in the road, and others spread leafy branches which they had cut from the fields. ⁹ Those who went in front and those who followed were shouting:

"Hosanna! Blessed is He who comes in the name of the Lord; ¹⁰ Blessed is the coming kingdom of our father David; Hosanna in the highest!"

¹¹ Jesus entered Jerusalem and came into the temple; and after looking around at everything, He left for Bethany with the twelve, since it was already late.

¹² On the next day, when they had left Bethany, He became hungry.

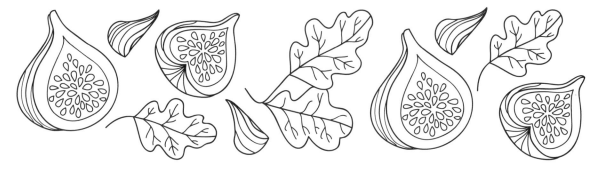

Fanfare surrounds Jesus' arrival into Jerusalem. Leafy branches rush through the air. Thick robes line the path, padding the clickity-clack of colt hooves.

The remarkable day arrives. Jesus makes His triumphal entry. Prophesies fulfilled. Praise unleashes. Divine royalty enters the scene.

But the Gospel of Mark won't let us forget Jesus' humanity. The very next day: "He became hungry."

Those are words pause-worthy. They remind us of a similar expression of Christ's humanity:

"Jesus wept" (John 11:35).

He became hungry reminds us Jesus took on flesh, like us.
He became hungry reminds us Jesus remains with us in our appetites and rumblings.
He became hungry reminds us Jesus comes alongside us in our pangs and pains.

Jesus became hungry, became human, to satisfy our deepest longings.

1. What encouragement do you find from reflecting on Jesus' humanity?
2. What part of your humanness needs Jesus most right now?
3. Using the Color Method, what stood out to you most from today's Scripture?
4. How has using the Color Method changed the way you've read Scripture?

WHEN SEASONS CHANGE
Day 27 - Mark 11:13-33 CSB

13 Seeing in the distance a fig tree with leaves, he went to find out if there was anything on it. When he came to it, he found nothing but leaves; for it was not the season for figs. 14 He said to it, "May no one ever eat fruit from you again!" And his disciples heard it.

15 They came to Jerusalem, and he went into the temple and began to throw out those buying and selling. He overturned the tables of the money changers and the chairs of those selling doves, 16 and would not permit anyone to carry goods through the temple. 17 He was teaching them: "Is it not written, My house will be called a house of prayer for all nations? But you have made it a den of thieves!"

18 The chief priests and the scribes heard it and started looking for a way to kill him. For they were afraid of him, because the whole crowd was astonished by his teaching. 19 Whenever evening came, they would go out of the city.

20 Early in the morning, as they were passing by, they saw the fig tree withered from the roots up. 21 Then Peter remembered and said to him, "Rabbi, look! The fig tree that you cursed has withered."

22 Jesus replied to them, "Have faith in God. 23 Truly I tell you, if anyone says to this mountain, 'Be lifted up and thrown into the sea,' and does not doubt in his heart, but believes that what

he says will happen, it will be done for him. ²⁴ Therefore I tell you, everything you pray and ask for—believe that you have received it and it will be yours. ²⁵ And whenever you stand praying, if you have anything against anyone, forgive him, so that your Father in heaven will also forgive you your wrongdoing."

²⁷ They came again to Jerusalem. As he was walking in the temple, the chief priests, the scribes, and the elders came ²⁸ and asked him, "By what authority are you doing these things? Who gave you this authority to do these things?"

²⁹ Jesus said to them, "I will ask you one question; then answer me, and I will tell you by what authority I do these things. ³⁰ Was John's baptism from heaven or of human origin? Answer me."

³¹ They discussed it among themselves: "If we say, 'From heaven,' he will say, 'Then why didn't you believe him?' ³² But if we say, 'Of human origin'"—they were afraid of the crowd, because everyone thought that John was truly a prophet. ³³ So they answered Jesus, "We don't know." And Jesus said to them, "Neither will I tell you by what authority I do these things."

Today's reading features a fig sandwich. Jesus becomes hungry on the way to the temple. He eyes a fruitless fig tree. Jesus says, "May no one ever eat fruit from you again!" Either Jesus is unaware of the seasons or the fig tree is symbolic of something more.

Soon the temple becomes a tumult. Tables flip and salesmen soon skedaddle. The chaotic scene erupts, but it too is symbolic of something more.

Then Jesus and the disciples cross the fig tree again. Peter notes the withering. Jesus leverages the moment and the upcoming interaction with the religious leaders to teach on authority. Perhaps the whole dialogue symbolizes something even more remarkable:

Sometimes old things must die so Christ can make things new.

These divine interactions involve more than fig trees and table flips. This is Jesus revealing Himself. Just as the fig tree is out of season, so too the season of the temple has passed. It will no longer produce fruit as the place where the ritual system of forgiveness happens. A new season has arrived with Christ as the ultimate authority, the ultimate sacrifice, and his temple will be a house of prayer for all nations.

1. Within the text, how do you see Jesus revealing Himself?
2. In what areas are you experiencing Jesus making all things new?
3. In what areas do you want Jesus to make all things new?
4. Using the Color Method, what stood out to you most from today's Scripture?

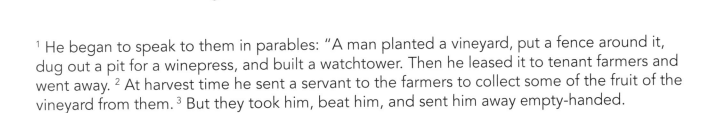

[1] He began to speak to them in parables: "A man planted a vineyard, put a fence around it, dug out a pit for a winepress, and built a watchtower. Then he leased it to tenant farmers and went away. [2] At harvest time he sent a servant to the farmers to collect some of the fruit of the vineyard from them. [3] But they took him, beat him, and sent him away empty-handed.

[4] Again he sent another servant to them, and they hit him on the head and treated him shamefully. [5] Then he sent another, and they killed that one. He also sent many others; some they beat, and others they killed. [6] He still had one to send, a beloved son. Finally he sent him to them, saying, 'They will respect my son.' [7] But those tenant farmers said to one another, 'This is the heir. Come, let's kill him, and the inheritance will be ours.' [8] So they seized him, killed him, and threw him out of the vineyard.

[9] What then will the owner of the vineyard do? He will come and kill the farmers and give the vineyard to others. [10] Haven't you read this Scripture: The stone that the builders rejected has become the cornerstone. [11] This came about from the Lord and is wonderful in our eyes?"

[12] They were looking for a way to arrest him but feared the crowd because they knew he had spoken this parable against them. So they left him and went away.

Based on a beautiful song in Isaiah 5:1-7, Jesus tells a prophetic parable. A landlord sends his servants and managers to collect rent and the tenants refuse to pay. The story escalates from sending the servants home empty-handed to shaming to torturing to murdering. The tale tailspins to disgust for the listeners.

The landlord decides to send his most precious child, reasoning that surely the tenants will respect his son's presence and authority. Yet they mutilate his body too, even refusing to bury him—an especially outrageous insult in Jewish culture.

The tale infuriates its listeners, especially the religious establishment, who are indicted by the parable. But Jesus ensures they don't miss the point. He quotes Psalm 118:22, "The stone that the builders rejected has become the cornerstone." The Hebrew word for "stone," *eben*, sounds much like the word for "son," *ben*. The rejected stone is the rejected son. Jesus is the new cornerstone.

Though spoken against the hard-hearted religious leaders, the underlying story reveals God's tender heart toward us. Did you notice how many times God keeps sending messengers, reaching out, refusing to let go? It's remarkable. God does that for us, too.

God shows up when we mess up.

Perhaps that's one reason Jesus encourages us to hear and listen so much. That we would be those who respond in obedience, who don't miss an opportunity to love, who are quick to change our ways and embrace God's grace.

1. When have you been hard-hearted like the tenants?
2. What does this story reveal to you about the nature of God's love?
3. Where have you experienced snapshots of grace this week?
4. Using the Color Method, what stood out to you most from today's Scripture?

HOW TO GET LIFE RIGHT EVERY TIME
Day 29 - Mark 12:13-34 NKJV

13 Then they sent to Him some of the Pharisees and the Herodians, to catch Him in His words. 14 When they had come, they said to Him, "Teacher, we know that You are true, and care about no one; for You do not regard the person of men, but teach the way of God in truth. Is it lawful to pay taxes to Caesar, or not?

15 Shall we pay, or shall we not pay?"

But He, knowing their hypocrisy, said to them, "Why do you test Me? Bring Me a denarius that I may see it." 16 So they brought it.

And He said to them, "Whose image and inscription is this?" They said to Him, "Caesar's." [17] And Jesus answered and said to them, "Render to Caesar the things that are Caesar's, and to God the things that are God's." And they marveled at Him.

[18] Then some Sadducees, who say there is no resurrection, came to Him; and they asked Him, saying: [19] "Teacher, Moses wrote to us that if a man's brother dies, and leaves his wife behind, and leaves no children, his brother should take his wife and raise up offspring for his brother.

[20] Now there were seven brothers. The first took a wife; and dying, he left no offspring. [21] And the second took her, and he died; nor did he leave any offspring. And the third likewise. [22] So the seven had her and left no offspring. Last of all the woman died also. [23] Therefore, in the resurrection, when they rise, whose wife will she be? For all seven had her as wife."

[24] Jesus answered and said to them, "Are you not therefore mistaken, because you do not know the Scriptures nor the power of God?

[25] For when they rise from the dead, they neither marry nor are given in marriage, but are like angels in heaven.

[26] But concerning the dead, that they rise, have you not read in the book of Moses, in the burning bush passage, how God spoke to him, saying, 'I am the God of Abraham, the God of Isaac, and the God of Jacob'?

[27] He is not the God of the dead, but the God of the living. You are therefore greatly mistaken."

[28] Then one of the scribes came, and having heard them reasoning together, perceiving that He had answered them well, asked Him, "Which is the first commandment of all?"

[29] Jesus answered him, "The first of all the commandments is: 'Hear, O Israel, the Lord our God, the Lord is one. [30] And you shall love the Lord your God with all your heart, with all your soul, with all your mind, and with all your strength.' This is the first commandment.

[31] And the second, like it, is this: 'You shall love your neighbor as yourself.' There is no other commandment greater than these."

[32] So the scribe said to Him, "Well said, Teacher. You have spoken the truth, for there is one God, and there is no other but He.

[33] And to love Him with all the heart, with all the understanding, with all the soul, and with all the strength, and to love one's neighbor as oneself, is more than all the whole burnt offerings and sacrifices."

[34] Now when Jesus saw that he answered wisely, He said to him, "You are not far from the kingdom of God." But after that no one dared question Him.

Surrounded by Pharisees, Sadducees, and scribes, Jesus becomes the next contestant on "Religious Jeopardy." The pietistic leaders pepper Him with dicey questions and examine Him with outlandish scenarios. Jesus wins every round.

One scribe stands out from the crowd when he asks what commandment should get top billing?

Jesus says, "Hear, O Israel!"

We could stop with those words. Listening to God is everything (see Day 20). Yet Jesus says to love God with every ventricle of your heart, every emotion of your soul, every synapse of your brain, every fiber of your muscles.

But the scribe takes Jesus' words one-step further when he notes that loving God with everything is greater than all the offerings and sacrifices.

Jesus declares the scribe a winner, "You are not far from the kingdom of God."

The Remarkable One teaches us that the kingdom of God draws near not when we ace an eschatology test, maintain perfect attendance at church functions, or write checks with lots of zeroes (though good theology, involvement in a faith community, and generosity are all wondrous):

People who get love right get life right.

The kingdom of God draws near when we love, love, love. When we walk in patience and humility. Keep no record of wrongs. Put others before ourselves. Practice grace and peace. Celebrate others. Bear, believe, hope, and endure all things.

1. Which religious rules do you practice that prevent you from loving others?
2. Who is the hardest-to-love person in your life right now?
3. What specific steps can you take to love that person this week?
4. Using the Color Method, what stood out to you most from today's Scripture?

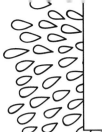

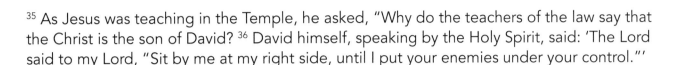

35 As Jesus was teaching in the Temple, he asked, "Why do the teachers of the law say that the Christ is the son of David? 36 David himself, speaking by the Holy Spirit, said: 'The Lord said to my Lord, "Sit by me at my right side, until I put your enemies under your control."'

37 David himself calls the Christ 'Lord,' so how can the Christ be his son?" The large crowd listened to Jesus with pleasure.

38 Jesus continued teaching and said, "Beware of the teachers of the law. They like to walk around wearing fancy clothes, and they love for people to greet them with respect in the marketplaces. 39 They love to have the most important seats in the synagogues and at feasts. 40 But they cheat widows and steal their houses and then try to make themselves look good by saying long prayers. They will receive a greater punishment."

41 Jesus sat near the Temple money box and watched the people put in their money. Many rich people gave large sums of money. 42 Then a poor widow came and put in two small copper coins, which were only worth a few cents.

43 Calling his followers to him, Jesus said, "I tell you the truth, this poor widow gave more than all those rich people. 44 They gave only what they did not need. This woman is very poor, but she gave all she had; she gave all she had to live on."

Just after He commends one of the scribes, He takes aim at them. Jesus doesn't mince words when warning about religious leaders. He cautions us against using religion to make ourselves famous instead of making our God famous.

Jesus expresses concern for widows then commends one particular widow.

This woman, in the midst of the clanging of generous donations, approaches the temple offering with two paper-thin coins. The kind that when they enter the offertory don't make a sound at all as they hit the metal offering collection.

Yet Jesus heralds her as the most remarkably generous of all because, while everyone else gave out of their extreme excess, she gave out of her great lack.

When you experience grace, you'll give with gratitude.

Her exceptional gift challenges us to be exceptional givers. We are meant to be people who rehearse gratitude and practice giving everywhere we go.

The greatest givers are grateful givers.

You don't need any fanfare for what you give, you simply need to remember how Jesus delights in your gifts. When you give, Jesus leans in and celebrates His work in you.

1. How can you rehearse thankfulness in your life?
2. What would exceptional giving look like for you?
3. Who is one person whose life would be changed by your generous gift?
4. Using the Color Method, what stood out to you most from today's Scripture?

WHY JESUS WARNS OF THE END TIMES
Day 31 - Mark 13:1-23 NIV

[1] As Jesus was leaving the temple, one of his disciples said to him, "Look, Teacher! What massive stones! What magnificent buildings!"

[2] "Do you see all these great buildings?" replied Jesus. "Not one stone here will be left on another; every one will be thrown down."

[3] As Jesus was sitting on the Mount of Olives opposite the temple, Peter, James, John and Andrew asked him privately, [4] "Tell us, when will these things happen? And what will be the sign that they are all about to be fulfilled?"

[5] Jesus said to them: "Watch out that no one deceives you. [6] Many will come in my name, claiming, 'I am he,' and will deceive many. [7] When you hear of wars and rumors of wars, do not be alarmed. Such things must happen, but the end is still to come. [8] Nation will rise against nation, and kingdom against kingdom. There will be earthquakes in various places, and famines. These are the beginning of birth pains.

[9] "You must be on your guard. You will be handed over to the local councils and flogged in the synagogues. On account of me you will stand before governors and kings as witnesses to them. [10] And the gospel must first be preached to all nations. [11] Whenever you are arrested and brought to trial, do not worry beforehand about what to say. Just say whatever is given you at the time, for it is not you speaking, but the Holy Spirit.

¹² "Brother will betray brother to death, and a father his child. Children will rebel against their parents and have them put to death. ¹³ Everyone will hate you because of me, but the one who stands firm to the end will be saved.

¹⁴ "When you see 'the abomination that causes desolation' standing where it does not belong—let the reader understand—then let those who are in Judea flee to the mountains. ¹⁵ Let no one on the housetop go down or enter the house to take anything out. ¹⁶ Let no one in the field go back to get their cloak. ¹⁷ How dreadful it will be in those days for pregnant women and nursing mothers! ¹⁸ Pray that this will not take place in winter, ¹⁹ because those will be days of distress unequaled from the beginning, when God created the world, until now—and never to be equaled again.

²⁰ "If the Lord had not cut short those days, no one would survive. But for the sake of the elect, whom he has chosen, he has shortened them. ²¹ At that time if anyone says to you, 'Look, here is the Messiah!' or, 'Look, there he is!' do not believe it. ²² For false messiahs and false prophets will appear and perform signs and wonders to deceive, if possible, even the elect. ²³ So be on your guard; I have told you everything ahead of time.

Jesus, known for heralding Good News, broadcasts hard news.

Deceivers will ransack souls. Famed structures will crumble.
Earthquakes will topple buildings. Famines will steal lives.
Believers will be macheted, shot, buried in mass graves.

All of these have come, will come, and fill our headlines today.

Yet tucked into Jesus' words is a remarkable promise: When we don't know what to say, the Holy Spirit will speak for us (Mark 13:11). Why is that so crucial?

The worst of times can become the most remarkable of times through Christ.

Jesus even forewarns us that these things will happen. Why?

Because the worst of times can become the most remarkable of times through Christ with us.

We do not need to be afraid—of today's trials or the trials to come. Why?

Because the worst of times can become the most remarkable of times through Christ with us.

1. Where in Mark 13:1-23 do you see Christ is with us?
2. When are you most tempted to forget Christ is with you?
3. How is Jesus showing love by sharing these things?
4. Using the Color Method, what stood out to you most from today's Scripture?

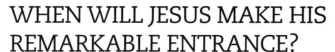
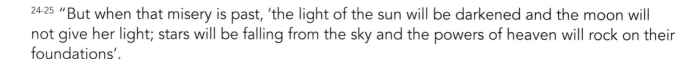
24-25 "But when that misery is past, 'the light of the sun will be darkened and the moon will not give her light; stars will be falling from the sky and the powers of heaven will rock on their foundations'.

26-27 Then men shall see the Son of Man coming in the clouds with great power and glory.

And then shall he send out his angels to summon his chosen together from every quarter, from furthest earth to highest heaven.

28-33 "Let the fig-tree illustrate this for you: when its branches grow tender and produce leaves, you know that summer is near, at your very doors!

I tell you that this generation will not have passed until all these things have come true.

Earth and sky will pass away, but what I have told you will never pass away!

But no one knows the day or the hour of this happening, not even the angels in Heaven, no, not even the Son—only the Father.

Keep your eyes open, keep on the alert, for you do not know when the time will be.

34-37 It is as if a man who is travelling abroad had left his house and handed it over to be managed by his servants.

He has given each one his work to do and has ordered the doorkeeper to be on the look-out for his return.

Just so must you keep a look-out, for you do not know when the master of the house will come—it might be late evening, or midnight, or cock-crow, or early morning—otherwise he might come unexpectedly and find you sound asleep.

What I am saying to you I am saying to all; keep on the alert!"

Jesus speaks of the shadows of things to come. Allusions. Mysteries. Hidden secrets that theologians and the church have tried to decode for thousands of years. Centuries of people have declared we are in the end times. They weren't wrong. Their time did end, but maybe not in the way they guessed.

Jesus warns that the stars will fall from the sky, and the heavenly bodies will be shaken. A reversal of creation will take place. Then Jesus will appear. In the meantime, Jesus says:

Keep alert. Stay alert. Be alert. Watch. Watch. Watch.

No one knows the day or hour of Christ's return but…

Every day is a day for Christ's remarkable entrance.

This is true in our hearts and lives and families and relationships and neighborhoods and work and finances. Christ isn't waiting to burst in your life one day or someday, but today. Live alert for Him.

1. Do you tend to look more for Christ's arrival someday or today? Explain.
2. How has Christ made a grand entrance in your life in the last three months?
3. Has your faith strengthened or wobbled by studying the end times? Explain.
4. Using the Color Method, what stood out to you most from today's Scripture?

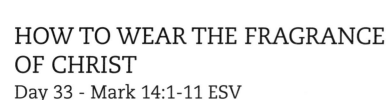

¹ It was now two days before the Passover and the Feast of Unleavened Bread.

And the chief priests and the scribes were seeking how to arrest him by stealth and kill him, ² for they said, "Not during the feast, lest there be an uproar from the people."

³ And while he was at Bethany in the house of Simon the leper, as he was reclining at table, a woman came with an alabaster flask of ointment of pure nard, very costly, and she broke the flask and poured it over his head.

⁴ There were some who said to themselves indignantly, "Why was the ointment wasted like that?

⁵ For this ointment could have been sold for more than three hundred denarii and given to the poor."

And they scolded her.

⁶ But Jesus said, "Leave her alone. Why do you trouble her?

She has done a beautiful thing to me.

⁷ For you always have the poor with you, and whenever you want, you can do good for them. But you will not always have me.

⁸ She has done what she could; she has anointed my body beforehand for burial.

⁹ And truly, I say to you, wherever the gospel is proclaimed in the whole world, what she has done will be told in memory of her."

¹⁰ Then Judas Iscariot, who was one of the twelve, went to the chief priests in order to betray him to them.

¹¹ And when they heard it, they were glad and promised to give him money.

And he sought an opportunity to betray him.

As the Passover approaches, the chief priests want to seize Jesus, but one woman wants to serve Jesus. A woman douses Jesus with perfume, staining the floor and filling the house with the scent.

In ancient times, you could purchase the knockoff nard, the equivalent of a fake Rolex or Coach bag, for only a hundred denarii a pound, but Scripture says the woman uses "pure nard," meaning without additives. She gives her very best, costing her an entire year's salary.

Long after the moment passes, the scent of her affection lingers. That scent follows Jesus as He enters Jerusalem. That smell drifts as Jesus distributes bread and wine during the Lord's Supper. That aroma likely emerges when He washes His disciples' feet—rubbing off on their bodies, when He delivers the last discourse, when He stands before Pilate, when gravity crushes His body.

But that remarkable scent doesn't just follow Jesus—it follows her.

The fragrance of divine affection follows those who love Christ.

What is this signature scent you carry as a follower of Jesus? Perhaps if we had to give the perfume a name, we'd call it "Remarkable."

1. Who has shared the fragrance of Christ with you recently?
2. How does loving Christ help you love others more?
3. What can you do today to express loving worship to God today?
4. Using the Color Method, what stood out to you most from today's Scripture?

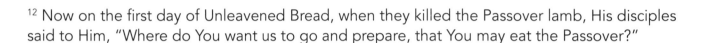

12 Now on the first day of Unleavened Bread, when they killed the Passover lamb, His disciples said to Him, "Where do You want us to go and prepare, that You may eat the Passover?"

13 And He sent out two of His disciples and said to them, "Go into the city, and a man will meet you carrying a pitcher of water; follow him. 14 Wherever he goes in, say to the master of the house, 'The Teacher says, "Where is the guest room in which I may eat the Passover with My disciples?"' 15 Then he will show you a large upper room, furnished and prepared; there make ready for us."

16 So His disciples went out, and came into the city, and found it just as He had said to them; and they prepared the Passover.

17 In the evening He came with the twelve. 18 Now as they sat and ate, Jesus said, "Assuredly, I say to you, one of you who eats with Me will betray Me."

19 And they began to be sorrowful, and to say to Him one by one, "Is it I?" And another said, "Is it I?" 20 He answered and said to them, "It is one of the twelve, who dips with Me in the dish. 21 The Son of Man indeed goes just as it is written of Him, but woe to that man by whom the Son of Man is betrayed! It would have been good for that man if he had never been born."

22 And as they were eating, Jesus took bread, blessed and broke it, and gave it to them and said, "Take, eat; this is My body."

23 Then He took the cup, and when He had given thanks He gave it to them, and they all drank from it. 24 And He said to them, "This is My blood of the new covenant, which is shed for many. 25 Assuredly, I say to you, I will no longer drink of the fruit of the vine until that day when I drink it new in the kingdom of God." 26 And when they had sung a hymn, they went out to the Mount of Olives.

27 Then Jesus said to them, "All of you will be made to stumble because of Me this night, for it is written: 'I will strike the Shepherd, and the sheep will be scattered.' 28 "But after I have been raised, I will go before you to Galilee."

29 Peter said to Him, "Even if all are made to stumble, yet I will not be." 30 Jesus said to him, "Assuredly, I say to you that today, even this night, before the rooster crows twice, you will deny Me three times." 31 But he spoke more vehemently, "If I have to die with You, I will not deny You!" And they all said likewise.

Mark 14 opens with the chief priests and teachers of the law scheming. While they plot, Jesus reclines at a table appearing unaffected.

In this relaxed, La-Z-Boy posture, a woman approaches and shatters a jar, disturbing the entire room. She baptizes Jesus in the scent of sweet affection and wild generosity, an act of burial preparation few comprehend.

Then Jesus sends a pair of disciples to prepare for Passover.

Now look closer.

A woman sacrifices much with her alabaster.
A man sacrifices much giving up his upper room.
Jesus sacrifices everything for all.

With each step, Jesus draws closer to giving all of Himself for all of us. In the process, Jesus teaches us:

Self-sacrifice is always significant.

Sometimes a sacrifice can seem rather unremarkable in the moment. A special gift. Some extra room. Giving up your place in line. Sending a thoughtful gift. Yet God takes joy in each one and uses them to display His glory.

1. Describe a time when someone else's sacrifice has made a significant impact on you.

2. Describe a time when your sacrifice has made a significant impact.

3. Are you more concerned with the heart behind or the size of your sacrifices?

4. Using the Color Method, what stood out to you most from today's Scripture?

THE BEST GIFT YOU CAN GIVE TO GOD
Day 35 - Mark 14:32-52 NIV

32 They went to a place called Gethsemane, and Jesus said to his disciples, "Sit here while I pray." 33 He took Peter, James and John along with him, and he began to be deeply distressed and troubled. 34 "My soul is overwhelmed with sorrow to the point of death," he said to them. "Stay here and keep watch."

35 Going a little farther, he fell to the ground and prayed that if possible the hour might pass from him. 36 "Abba, Father," he said, "everything is possible for you. Take this cup from me. Yet not what I will, but what you will."

37 Then he returned to his disciples and found them sleeping. "Simon," he said to Peter, "are you asleep? Couldn't you keep watch for one hour? 38 Watch and pray so that you will not fall into temptation. The spirit is willing, but the flesh is weak."

39 Once more he went away and prayed the same thing. 40 When he came back, he again found them sleeping, because their eyes were heavy. They did not know what to say to him.

41 Returning the third time, he said to them, "Are you still sleeping and resting? Enough! The hour has come. Look, the Son of Man is delivered into the hands of sinners. 42 Rise! Let us go! Here comes my betrayer!"

43 Just as he was speaking, Judas, one of the Twelve, appeared. With him was a crowd armed with swords and clubs, sent from the chief priests, the teachers of the law, and the elders.

44 Now the betrayer had arranged a signal with them: "The one I kiss is the man; arrest him and lead him away under guard."

45 Going at once to Jesus, Judas said, "Rabbi!" and kissed him. 46 The men seized Jesus and arrested him. 47 Then one of those standing near drew his sword and struck the servant of the high priest, cutting off his ear.

48 "Am I leading a rebellion," said Jesus, "that you have come out with swords and clubs to capture me? 49 Every day I was with you, teaching in the temple courts, and you did not arrest me. But the Scriptures must be fulfilled."

50 Then everyone deserted him and fled. 51 A young man, wearing nothing but a linen garment, was following Jesus. When they seized him, 52 he fled naked, leaving his garment behind.

The disciples have watched Jesus disappear up hills and mountainsides to talk with the Father many times before. This time Jesus insists a trio—Peter, James, and John—accompany Him.

Perhaps Peter hopes he'll catch a glimpse of another transfiguration, slipping his cell phone in his back pocket for any #selfie opportunities. Instead, they witness a different transformation. Jesus' expression morphs before their eyes.

The countenance of the Remarkable One they adore darkens. With furrowed brow and a tight jaw, Jesus confesses, "My soul is overwhelmed with sorrow to the point of death."

Then He makes a request: "Stay here and keep watch with me."

The disciples are already confused by the day's events, their bodies exhausted from travel. Jesus' groans and cries fade as they enter snoredom.

Jesus returns and nudges them: "Watch and pray."

Though the Scripture doesn't record these words, the underlying suggestion is, "I need you now. I need *you* with Me."

Yet His friends, His closest friends, nod off again. They're too sleepy to do what He's asked of them.

What strikes me most about this story is that Jesus wants His closest disciples *with* Him. He could have gone to Gethsemane alone. He'd climbed countless hills and mounts on His own. Yet this night, He wants them *with* Him—awake, alert, praying.

Jesus asks the disciples to give the gift He gives us:

The gift of presence.

They missed it. And sometimes we do, too. But never forget:

The gift of presence is the best gift you can give God.

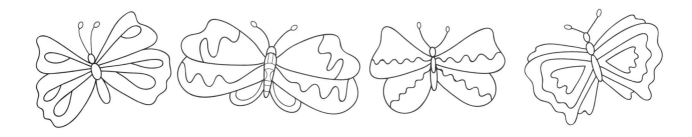

1. Why do you think Jesus selected this trio to go with Him?
2. When are you most likely to nod off to God's presence?
3. What can you do today to be fully present with Jesus?
4. Using the Color Method, what stood out to you most from today's Scripture?

53 And they led Jesus to the high priest. And all the chief priests and the elders and the scribes came together. 54 And Peter had followed him at a distance, right into the courtyard of the high priest. And he was sitting with the guards and warming himself at the fire.

55 Now the chief priests and the whole council were seeking testimony against Jesus to put him to death, but they found none. 56 For many bore false witness against him, but their testimony did not agree.

57 And some stood up and bore false witness against him, saying, 58 "We heard him say, 'I will destroy this temple that is made with hands, and in three days I will build another, not made with hands.'" 59 Yet even about this their testimony did not agree.

60 And the high priest stood up in the midst and asked Jesus, "Have you no answer to make? What is it that these men testify against you?" 61 But he remained silent and made no answer. Again the high priest asked him, "Are you the Christ, the Son of the Blessed?" 62 And Jesus said, "I am, and you will see the Son of Man seated at the right hand of Power, and coming with the clouds of heaven."

63 And the high priest tore his garments and said, "What further witnesses do we need? 64 You have heard his blasphemy. What is your decision?" And they all condemned him as deserving death. 65 And some began to spit on him and to cover his face and to strike him, saying to him, "Prophesy!" And the guards received him with blows.

66 And as Peter was below in the courtyard, one of the servant girls of the high priest came, 67 and seeing Peter warming himself, she looked at him and said, "You also were with the Nazarene, Jesus." 68 But he denied it, saying, "I neither know nor understand what you mean." And he went out into the gateway and the rooster crowed.

69 And the servant girl saw him and began again to say to the bystanders, "This man is one of them." 70 But again he denied it. And after a little while the bystanders again said to Peter, "Certainly you are one of them, for you are a Galilean."

71 But he began to invoke a curse on himself and to swear, "I do not know this man of whom you speak." 72 And immediately the rooster crowed a second time. And Peter remembered how Jesus had said to him, "Before the rooster crows twice, you will deny me three times."

And he broke down and wept.

Just a few hours before, Peter blurts that if everything falls apart and everyone else bails, he will remain. Jesus says, "Don't be so sure." But Peter is sure. "I'll never deny you!" he protests. All the other disciples say the same thing (Mark 14:29-31).

Never say never.

It's hard to watch Peter run from the cross without recognizing the ways we run, too.

Who wants to give up their dreams and desires?
Who wants to walk through the fire of obedience?
Who wants to enter the crucible of suffering?
Who wants to answer the call to come and die?

The cross has always appeared wonky, awkward—a place where pain trumps pleasure and sacrifice triumphs selfishness.

Yet Mark's placement of these episodes with Jesus' little Rocky, reminds us that proclaiming Jesus as the Messiah is only the first step to becoming a true follower. Then, hour by hour and inch by inch, we must give up our expectations of what we think the Remarkable One will do and be for us, to embrace who He really is and where He's really taking us.

At times, like Peter, we'll protest, because We. Don't. Want. To. Go. There.

The cross is the remarkable centerpiece where our will aligns with God's will.

Naturally, no one in their right mind would want to go there. Only those whose minds are aligned with Christ can embrace the cross.

1. When have you been ashamed of knowing Jesus?
2. In what ways can you relate to Peter's response?
3. What kinds of sacrifices do you sense Jesus nudging you toward?
4. Using the Color Method, what stood out to you most from today's Scripture?

¹ At dawn's first light, the high priests, with the religious leaders and scholars, arranged a conference with the entire Jewish Council.

After tying Jesus securely, they took him out and presented him to Pilate.

²⁻³ Pilate asked him, "Are you the 'King of the Jews'?" He answered, "If you say so." The high priests let loose a barrage of accusations.

⁴⁻⁵ Pilate asked again, "Aren't you going to answer anything? That's quite a list of accusations."

Still, he said nothing.

Pilate was impressed, really impressed.

⁶⁻¹⁰ It was a custom at the Feast to release a prisoner, anyone the people asked for.

There was one prisoner called Barabbas, locked up with the insurrectionists who had committed murder during the uprising against Rome.

As the crowd came up and began to present its petition for him to release a prisoner, Pilate anticipated them:

"Do you want me to release the King of the Jews to you?"

Pilate knew by this time that it was through sheer spite that the high priests had turned Jesus over to him.

¹¹⁻¹² But the high priests by then had worked up the crowd to ask for the release of Barabbas.

Pilate came back, "So what do I do with this man you call King of the Jews?"

¹³ They yelled, "Nail him to a cross!"

¹⁴ Pilate objected, "But for what crime?" But they yelled all the louder, "Nail him to a cross!"

¹⁵ Pilate gave the crowd what it wanted, set Barabbas free and turned Jesus over for whipping and crucifixion.

The road to the cross is lined with key characters and their actions. The disciples' desertion. Peter's denial. Pilate's questioning.

Now Barabbas appears. A rebel turned murderer, he resides on death row.

Barabbas' name can be translated as a "son of the father." The people literally choose between two sons of the father. And they couldn't be more different.

Jesus is innocent.
Barabbas is guilty.

Jesus leads many to life.
Barabbas leads many astray.

Jesus does nothing to deserve death.
Barabbas does everything to deserve death.

Jesus becomes the horrific and holy substitution for Barabbas and us. Like Barabbas, we are the guilty ones who deserve a death sentence. Yet Jesus takes the full brunt of punishment to give us new life.

The innocent is deemed a sinner so sinners can be deemed innocent.

Jesus exchanges our guilt for His innocence. Barabbas' physical release of freedom provides a foretaste of the remarkable freedom Jesus unleashes to us through the cross.

1. Where do you struggle with feeling guilty?
2. How does today's reading remind you of your innocence?
3. What do you imagine Barabbas thought when he was set free?
4. Using the Color Method, what stood out to you most from today's Scripture?

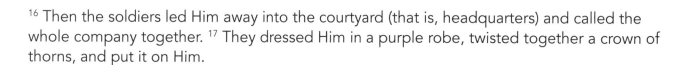

16 Then the soldiers led Him away into the courtyard (that is, headquarters) and called the whole company together. 17 They dressed Him in a purple robe, twisted together a crown of thorns, and put it on Him.

18 And they began to salute Him, "Hail, King of the Jews!" 19 They kept hitting Him on the head with a reed and spitting on Him. Getting down on their knees, they were paying Him homage. 20 When they had mocked Him, they stripped Him of the purple robe, put His clothes on Him, and led Him out to crucify Him.

21 They forced a man coming in from the country, who was passing by, to carry Jesus' cross. He was Simon, a Cyrenian, the father of Alexander and Rufus. 22 And they brought Jesus to the place called Golgotha (which means Skull Place).

23 They tried to give Him wine mixed with myrrh, but He did not take it. 24 Then they crucified Him and divided His clothes, casting lots for them to decide what each would get. 25 Now it was nine in the morning when they crucified Him. 26 The inscription of the charge written against Him was: THE KING OF THE JEWS.

27 They crucified two criminals with Him, one on His right and one on His left. 28 So the Scripture was fulfilled that says: And He was counted among outlaws. 29 Those who passed by were yelling insults at Him, shaking their heads, and saying, "Ha! The One who would demolish the sanctuary and build it in three days, 30 save Yourself by coming down from the cross!"

31 In the same way, the chief priests with the scribes were mocking Him to one another and saying, "He saved others; He cannot save Himself! 32 Let the Messiah, the King of Israel, come down now from the cross, so that we may see and believe." Even those who were crucified with Him were taunting Him.

33 When it was noon, darkness came over the whole land until three in the afternoon. 34 And at three Jesus cried out with a loud voice, "Eloi, Eloi, lemásabachtháni?" which is translated, "My God, My God, why have You forsaken Me?"

35 When some of those standing there heard this, they said, "Look, He's calling for Elijah!" 36 Someone ran and filled a sponge with sour wine, fixed it on a reed, offered Him a drink, and said, "Let's see if Elijah comes to take Him down!"

#RemarkableStudy

37 But Jesus let out a loud cry and breathed His last. 38 Then the curtain of the sanctuary was split in two from top to bottom. 39 When the centurion, who was standing opposite Him, saw the way He breathed His last, he said, "This man really was God's Son!"

40 There were also women looking on from a distance. Among them were Mary Magdalene, Mary the mother of James the younger and of Joses, and Salome. 41 When He was in Galilee, they would follow Him and help Him. Many other women had come up with Him to Jerusalem.

Darkness descends. A holy corpse hangs on boards. A sword slits flesh. Blood and water cascade in a mind-bending cosmic reality which fulfills the words of ancient prophecies.

Good Friday. The remarkable day when those who stand at the foot of the cross see nothing good.

The day the storm of heaven and hell crash into each other.
The day we recognize our true powerlessness.
The day the world goes dark.

No wonder we want to rush through Good Friday. We know how the story bends and how the story ends. We scramble toward the light.

Good Friday challenges us to slow our rushed hearts, embrace the stillness, and sit in the inky blackness.

To recall. To reflect. To remember.

And invite Christ in the deepest, darkest places in our souls. We don't need to be afraid of the dark when we remember:

God knows His way around the dark.

1. What are three reasons you're thankful for the stillness of Good Friday?
2. What is the weightiest part of Good Friday for you?
3. What's a dark place in your life into which you need to invite Christ?
4. Using the Color Method, what stood out to you most from today's Scripture?

WHEN IT'S STILL SATURDAY
Day 39 - Mark 15:42-47 CSB

⁴² When it was already evening, because it was the day of preparation (that is, the day before the Sabbath),

⁴³ Joseph of Arimathea, a prominent member of the Sanhedrin who was himself looking forward to the kingdom of God, came and boldly went to Pilate and asked for Jesus's body.

⁴⁴ Pilate was surprised that he was already dead. Summoning the centurion, he asked him whether he had already died.

⁴⁵ When he found out from the centurion, he gave the corpse to Joseph.

⁴⁶ After he bought some linen cloth, Joseph took him down and wrapped him in the linen.

Then he laid him in a tomb cut out of the rock and rolled a stone against the entrance to the tomb.

⁴⁷ Mary Magdalene and Mary the mother of Jesus were watching where he was laid.

#RemarkableStudy

The final days of Jesus' life are marked by much preparation.

The religious leaders are preparing.
The women are preparing.
The disciples are preparing.
Judas is preparing.
Jesus is preparing.

All the while, God is preparing the most remarkable caper of all time.

Remember, it's not Sunday yet. It's still Saturday.

Most of us live our lives wanting Resurrection Sunday apart from Good Friday and Sad Saturday. Sunday is joy and wonder and hope and new life. Friday and Saturday are torture and death and confusion and sadness. Who wants that?

We tell ourselves that God has a plan for our lives that doesn't involve Fridays or Saturdays. If we just…

pray hard enough…
live holy enough…
give to others enough…
fill-in-the-blank enough…

then Fridays and Saturdays might happen to others, but not us.

For millennia, we've burrowed for routes under the cross, slinked for ways around the cross, even developing schemes to climb over the cross. Some have even transformed the cross into a jungle gym.

We want breakthrough without being broken.
We want strength without suffering.
We want power without paying a price.

Good Friday and Sad Saturday remind us:

There are endless ways to skirt around the cross, but only one way through it.

Jesus beckons you to take up the cross, to enter the splintered timber, to walk through the crucible of affliction. As you pass through the heart of those wooden beams, you'll discover the depth of God's love for you, as well as the mystery that your capacity for loving God and loving others will expand beyond what you ever thought possible.

1. When have you tried to avoid the cross in the last month?
2. Describe a time when Christ revealed Himself to you in a dark time.
3. How did that experience impact your faith?
4. Using the Color Method, what stood out to you most from today's Scripture?

HE IS RISEN INDEED!
Day 40 - Mark 16:1-20 NKJV

¹ Now when the Sabbath was past, Mary Magdalene, Mary the mother of James, and Salome bought spices, that they might come and anoint Him. ² Very early in the morning, on the first day of the week, they came to the tomb when the sun had risen. ³ And they said among themselves, "Who will roll away the stone from the door of the tomb for us?"

⁴ But when they looked up, they saw that the stone had been rolled away—for it was very large. ⁵ And entering the tomb, they saw a young man clothed in a long white robe sitting on the right side; and they were alarmed.

⁶ But he said to them, "Do not be alarmed. You seek Jesus of Nazareth, who was crucified. He is risen! He is not here. See the place where they laid Him. ⁷ But go, tell His disciples—and Peter—that He is going before you into Galilee; there you will see Him, as He said to you."

⁸ So they went out quickly and fled from the tomb, for they trembled and were amazed. And they said nothing to anyone, for they were afraid.

⁹ Now when He rose early on the first day of the week, He appeared first to Mary Magdalene, out of whom He had cast seven demons. ¹⁰ She went and told those who had been with Him, as they mourned and wept. ¹¹ And when they heard that He was alive and had been seen by her, they did not believe.

¹² After that, He appeared in another form to two of them as they walked and went into the country. ¹³ And they went and told it to the rest, but they did not believe them either.

¹⁴ Later He appeared to the eleven as they sat at the table; and He rebuked their unbelief and hardness of heart, because they did not believe those who had seen Him after He had risen. ¹⁵ And He said to them, "Go into all the world and preach the gospel to every creature. ¹⁶ He who believes and is baptized will be saved; but he who does not believe will be condemned.

¹⁷ And these signs will follow those who believe: In My name they will cast out demons; they will speak with new tongues; ¹⁸ they will take up serpents; and if they drink anything deadly, it will by no means hurt them; they will lay hands on the sick, and they will recover."

¹⁹ So then, after the Lord had spoken to them, He was received up into heaven, and sat down at the right hand of God. ²⁰ And they went out and preached everywhere, the Lord working with them and confirming the word through the accompanying signs. Amen.

#RemarkableStudy

Resurrection Day is the remarkable miracle of all Jesus has done and all He has called us to do.

The Remarkable One calls us to live as people who can't keep the Good News to ourselves. We have the privilege of sharing Jesus with our neighbors and friends, companions and acquaintances. We are meant to live on high alert for opportunities to share Jesus, to be like Jesus, to radiate Jesus.

The resurrection of Christ is the resurrection in us.

The resurrection calls each of us to be conduits of the Jesus-life, proclaiming His words, His acts, His power.

This is who we are. The people of God. The followers of Jesus. The church. Those who gather around the table to talk, encourage, pray, sing, and share contagious joy as children of God.

My hope and prayer is that the Remarkable One will complete the remarkable work He has begun in you.

1. What theme has resonated in you as you've read through the Gospel of Mark?
2. Which day's reading has been the most transformative for you?
3. Which day's reading has been the most challenging for you?
4. Using the Color Method, what stood out to you most from today's Scripture?

Lovelies Just for You

Fight Back With Joy

Through vulnerable storytelling, a difficult diagnosis, and a good dose of humor, Fight Back With Joy reveals how joy is more than whimsy. It's the weapon you can use to fight life's battles.

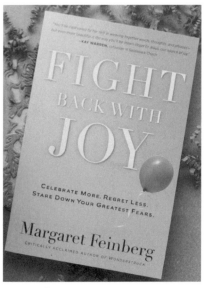

What to Say When You Don't Know What to Say Greeting Cards

These modern, bright n' beautiful cards are made to encourage and inspire. All are designed to equip you to help those facing tough times fight back with joy.

Flourish: 52-Week Devotional

Flourish offers a year of weekly devotions that will awaken your soul to a life of fullness and joy that spills over to bless others.

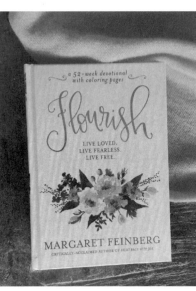

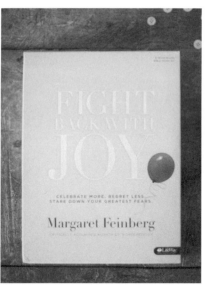

Fight Back With Joy: 6-Session DVD Bible Study

Dive deep into the Scripture in order to expand your joy threshold, beat back discouragement, and awaken God's fierce love for you. You'll be equipped with more than two dozen tactics to begin to fight back with joy no matter what battleground you're on.

Visit margaretfeinberg.com to find fresh Bible studies, When You Don't Know What to Say cards, and Scripture-based coloring books.